THE DANDELION INSURRECTION
STUDY GUIDE

- making change through nonviolent action -

by Rivera Sun

The Dandelion Insurrection Study Guide

- making change through nonviolent action -

Rising Sun Press Works
P.O. Box 1751, El Prado, NM 87529

Library of Congress Control Number:
2015930941

ISBN 978-0-9848132-78
Sun, Rivera 1982-
The Dandelion Insurrection Study Guide

For Dandelions, everywhere!

Table of Contents

THE DANDELION INSURRECTION
STUDY GUIDE

- making change through nonviolent action -

Rivera Sun reading from The Dandelion Insurrection before a strategic nonviolent action workshop in Madrid, New Mexico. Photo by Shelly Johnson.

Dear Friends,

The most common question readers send me is: *how do we make The Dandelion Insurrection real?*

In these times of turbulent change, when our water, air, land, and livelihoods are being threatened; when democracy is a dream and nothing more; when our military-industrial complex perpetuates endless war; when the brutality of police threatens people across the nation; and when even the continuation of life on Earth is uncertain . . . in these times, asking how to bring to life a novel that depicts ordinary, extraordinary people rising up in a nonviolent struggle for life, liberty, and love is a serious question. It deserves a serious response.

This study guide is my reply.

The greatest stories are the ones that change our lives. In writing a study guide to *The Dandelion Insurrection*, my hope is to reveal this as a novel based not on pure fantasy and conjecture, but on careful research and consideration of nonviolent struggles that have taken place around the world. The intention of this study guide is to share the tools of nonviolent action in a way that inspires you to use them to make change. You see, when the roof leaks, the hammer does no good sitting in the toolbox. Likewise, in these times of great change, nonviolent action should not stay between the covers of a novel. We must lift the story off the page and into our lives.

This study guide will illuminate and encourage discussion about how change is made through strategic nonviolent action. We will look at types of actions, levels of organization, dynamics, strategic planning, how to build a movement, personal choices and self-care, messaging, and more.

The guide is laid out in eight sessions that draw lessons from *The Dandelion Insurrection*. Historical examples of nonviolent struggles and discussion questions are included to give context to your reflections. Links to further resources are included both in the resources section and also within the study guide.

As an author and an activist, it is my hope that this study guide will serve you in your efforts to create a more equal, just, peaceful, and sustainable world.

With love,

Rivera Sun

How to Use This Study Guide

To use this guide, please read *The Dandelion Insurrection*. Not only is it a terrifically enjoyable story, it is also the basis for many lively discussions in these lessons. Gather a group of friends or students, or your book club, or peace and justice group; and encourage everyone to read the novel together and then engage with this study guide. You can find copies of both the novel and the study guide at www.riverasun.com

The study guide is designed to allow flexibility for both individual and group study, and is laid out in eight sessions. Each session takes about 1.5 or 2 hours. If you are meeting with a group, set a time to meet once a week. Read each section prior to the group session. Then, you can quickly review it as a group and begin the discussion questions or exercises. Where there is a discussion or exercise, you should choose someone to facilitate. Before the group gathers, this person should spend some time reading the exercise carefully and preparing the materials the group will need for the process.

As you read the novel, please remember that The Dandelion Insurrection is not a textbook on nonviolent struggle. Rather, the fictional story tries to reflect the reality of dynamic and powerful forces waging conflict. Sometimes, the Dandelion Insurrection takes the upper hand; other times, their opposition forces them to run for cover. Each side makes strategic mistakes, overlooks important considerations, and launches surprise attacks that catch the other side off guard. Planning and improvisation both play their roles in a struggle, but there is great importance and value in strategic planning. This type of analysis is like a muscle - the more you exercise it the stronger it is in times of emergency and improvisation.

In all of the discussions, readings, and exercises, this study guide is intended to help bridge fact and fiction, providing you with tools for making wise choices in your own journey.

Filmmaker Velcrow Ripper on NYC subway.

"In a time that looms around the corner of today, in a place on the edge of our nation, it is a crime to dissent, a crime to assemble, a crime to stand up for one's life. Despite all this – or perhaps, because of it – the Dandelion Insurrection began!"
– The Dandelion Insurrection

Session One: Introductions & Beginnings

Welcome! Through the course of this study guide, you will learn the basic dynamics of nonviolent struggle, how to craft strategy and campaigns, how to choose wise actions that help you reach your goals, how to bring people together, and how to choose slogans, messages, images, and ideas that inspire change throughout society!

For your first session, please read this section of the study guide before your study group gathers.

The Dandelion Insurrection Study Guide to making change through nonviolent action is a journey. In today's session, we'll start with our own stories. Next, we'll take a quick moment to share some thoughts on *The Dandelion Insurrection*. Then we'll look at some myths and truths of nonviolent action. Lastly, we'll explore the reasons why people choose to use nonviolent action.

Introductions
(Time: 5 mins)

Facilitators: To begin, invite everyone to share his or her name and a moment from The Dandelion Insurrection that was particularly evocative, poignant, or exciting for him or her. For instance, *"I'm Rivera Sun, and I found the cazerolazo – pots and pans banging – a really exciting idea to protest and break martial law."*

Discussion: Your Story
(Time: 35 mins)

Next, let's take a moment to reflect on our own experiences. If you are in a group, then this is a great opportunity to get to know one another more deeply. If you are studying on your own, these stories and questions serve as prompts for personal reflection and discovery.

Our stories (who we are, where we're from, how we grew up, what moves us into action, what pushes us away) are important for understanding how we think change is made. I'm going to start by sharing a small part of my own story, and then invite you and your group to share your stories with each other.

Facilitators: Check in with everyone to see if they had a chance to read the short story below. If not, perhaps give them a few moments to read it. Then, proceed to the discussion that follows the story.

Reading:
Late-bloomer - A Personal Journey Into Activism
by Rivera Sun

I grew up on an organic potato farm in Northern Maine with radical parents not unlike Bill Gray and Ellen Byrd. My four siblings and I worked hard as teenagers, harvesting potatoes, carrots, raspberries, strawberries, and other crops to be shipped to local and downstate markets. Although my family was deeply involved in the local food movement, I ignored politics and other social justice movements for nearly a decade. I had my reasons for my disenchantment: my first presidential election was in 2000, when the Supreme Court stopped the Florida vote count, and my second year of college saw the passing of the Patriot Act amidst widespread hysteria over terrorism. I saw our nation's entry into the Iraq War as despicable, facilitated by the blatant lies of greedy politicians, but I felt powerless to stop it. This feeling was reinforced when the massive public demonstrations against the war were utterly ignored by our elected leaders. I did not - and still do not - have much faith in electoral politics. For years, I warded off feelings of powerlessness by cultivating apathy to social and political injustice. I buried myself in my dance-theater work. I admired my activist friends, but did not become involved in many movements until I began writing social protest novels.

In the desert outside of Taos, New Mexico, I began researching for my second social protest novel, *The Dandelion Insurrection*. Since the plot posits a hidden corporate dictatorship, I decided to type in an Internet

Rivera Sun carrying giant Dolores Huerta puppet built by Jeanne Green and Marilyn Hoff. Photo by Dariel Garner.

search for the words "how to bring down a dictator nonviolently". Wow! Not only had nonviolent struggle ousted one dictator, it had ousted dozens! Even more significantly, scholars and organizers around the world had been hard at work studying, writing, and educating people on how to use nonviolent action to create tangible change in the world. I began reading and studying obsessively. With these tools in my hands, I was no longer afraid to build or participate in movements for change. As *The Dandelion Insurrection* came into this world, I also moved into action, playing a small role in many efforts, just one of the thousands of ordinary, extraordinary people like you and me who are working for justice and change.

Discussion: Your Story

Part One - Reflection

Facilitators: Invite participants to take out notebooks and pens. Let's start by taking 5 minutes of silence to reflect on the following questions:

- Who are you?
- Where did you come from?
- What challenges have you faced in your life, and today?
- What do you love?
- What moves you into action?
- What keeps you from taking action?

Scribble notes on these questions as you reflect on them. You do not need to have an answer to each question, nor a comprehensive answer to any of them. After taking this time to reflect, you'll be asked to share some of your reflections with the group.

Part Two - Sharing & Listening

Facilitators: After 5 minutes of quiet reflection, ring a small bell or gently let everyone know that it's time to share our reflections. Go around the group, giving each person a few minutes to share his or her story. If your group is very large, split into many small groups between 5-10 people. You may wish to use an egg timer and small bell to gently remind everyone to keep the sharing to a few minutes so each person has a chance to speak.

Listening is a powerful action. In sharing our stories, we are asked to listen to one another with non-judgmental minds. Our friends are not asking for our advice, opinions or critique of their stories. Our role is to listen fully. You may wish to invite the group to simply say "thank you" after each story is shared.

Active, non-judging listening is very important for building trust and honesty. Perhaps, like me, you're a late-blooming activist. Or maybe you've been at it since the day you were born. Some people are not sure they want to get involved in social justice movements . . . and that's okay. As we share our stories, the most important gift we can give one another is complete presence and non-judgmental listening. When I first became involved in activism, I was afraid of being judged for my decade of apathy. I feared that more seasoned activists would laugh at my ignorance, or that I would offend someone over issues of race, gender, sexuality, class, education, etc. When we respect one another, we have an opportunity to be real human beings with each other. Honesty can emerge, and from that, trust.

Go around the group, listening with an open mind and heart to the short stories about our journeys towards nonviolent movements for change. If your group feels hesitant to explore their stories, another way to approach this conversation is ask each other, how did you hear about *The Dandelion Insurrection*? What inspired you to read it?

Conclusion: Facilitators, please take a moment to thank your group for sharing their stories. If it feels appropriate, you may wish to invite comments or reflections about listening to the stories. When you feel complete, move on to the next section. We will be returning to personal reflections at several points throughout the study guide. Next, let's discuss *The Dandelion Insurrection*.

Discussion: The Dandelion Insurrection
(Time: 15-20mins)

Over these sessions, we will discuss the events in *The Dandelion Insurrection* in great detail, exploring historical nonviolent movements and the fictional depictions in the book. This discussion is a chance for the group to relate their reactions to the novel.

Facilitators: Decide whether you wish to use a talking stick, or go around in a circle giving everyone a chance to speak, or to open the conversation up for popcorn-style comments. You do not need to explore all the questions below. Use the ones that are most interesting to you or the group and adjust for the amount of time the group has.

Discussion Questions:

- How did you hear about the novel and what was your initial reaction to the title and description?
- What were some sections or moments that deeply excited you?
- What were some parts that presented new ideas or concepts to you?
- Were there any challenging moments in the novel or ideas that you disagreed with?
- What memories or reflections on real-life nonviolent struggles or contemporary issues did the novel evoke in you?
- What were some things that *The Dandelion Insurrection* has made you more curious to learn about?
- Could you imagine yourself as any of the characters in the book? Which one(s)? Why?
- If *The Dandelion Insurrection* were really happening would you be involved? Why or why not? And if so, in what ways would you be involved?

Conclusion: Facilitators, please thank everyone for their comments and let them know that next, we're going to look at some of the myths and truths about nonviolent action.

Discussion: Myths and Truths About Nonviolent Action
(Time: 20mins)

Facilitators: To refresh everyone's memories about *The Myths and Truths of Nonviolent Action*, invite each person to read a myth and summarize the truth in his or her own words. After reading the myths and truths, the group can move into the discussion. You will find the discussion questions below the reading.

Reading: Myths and Truths About Nonviolent Action

The plot of *The Dandelion Insurrection* is rooted in a nonviolent struggle to restore democracy in a United States that "looms around the corner of today". In writing the story, I wanted to honor the incredible struggles of people worldwide who have used nonviolent action to achieve social and political change. To do this, I had to do a lot of research . . . but it was the best kind of research! The more I learned, the more inspired I became. The feelings of powerlessness that I once felt were replaced by a sense of possibility. So many people around the world had made change through strategic nonviolent action . . . surely, we could too!

I also discovered that nonviolence means many things to many people. Sometimes it is a way of life or a personal practice or a type of conflict resolution or a style of communication. In the context of this study guide, I use the term, *nonviolent struggle* or *nonviolent action* to be clear that we are discussing a way of resolving conflicts without the use of physical violence.

Luke Sekera–Flanders at the People's Climate March in NYC, 2014, reading The Dandelion Insurrection. Photo by Nickie Sekera.

Throughout *The Dandelion Insurrection*, the characters make great change without the use of guns or physical violence. The novel shows many examples of methods of nonviolent action including strikes, boycotts, constructive programs, noncooperation, symbolic marches, vigils, rallies, walk-outs, shut-downs, blockades, and civil disobedience. Gene Sharp, a preeminent scholar of nonviolent struggle, identified 198 Methods of Nonviolent Struggle in 1973, adding that he believed many more existed and would be invented in the coming years. (You can find these methods in Appendix A.)

Nonviolent struggle has been used in numerous countries, including Estonia, Latvia, Lithuania, Poland, East Germany, Czechoslovakia, Slovenia, Madagascar, Serbia, Mali, Bolivia, the Philippines, Nepal, Zambia, South Korea, Chile, Argentina, Haiti, Brazil, Uruguay, Portugal, Malawi, Thailand, Bulgaria, Hungary, Nigeria, South Africa, the United States, Canada, Australia, the United Kingdom, Iran, Egypt, Tunisia, Ukraine,

Burma, France, Norway, Denmark, Sweden, India, and many others. Indeed, it may be easier to list the countries that have *not* used nonviolent struggle to try to achieve social and political changes.

Nonviolent action has brought down dictators, ousted tyrannical regimes, and won civil rights, independence, and self-rule. Nonviolent action has now been demonstrated to be twice as effective as violence in repelling foreign invasions, ending occupations, and changing a governmental regime. Despite this, numerous inaccuracies and myths about nonviolent action still circulate among our friends, neighbors, and family members. Let's take a look at some of them.

Myth: Nonviolence doesn't work.
Truth: When used wisely and strategically, nonviolence is often more effective than violence in achieving the objectives of the movement. As mentioned above, empirical studies have now demonstrated that nonviolent action is twice as effective as violence in repelling foreign invasions, ending occupations, and changing a governmental regime. (For more info on this, read Chenoweth and Stephan, *Why Civil Resistance Works.*) Sometimes, when people say nonviolent action doesn't work, they may lack information about the history of nonviolent action, or are equating the whole of nonviolent action with symbolic protests and petitions. Nonviolent action *does* work, often better than violence, especially if wise strategies are used.

Josie Lenwell and friend demonstrating against drones.

Myth: Nonviolence is passive and cowardly.
Truth: Exactly the opposite! Nonviolent action means taking courageous, committed action to make change using methods that do not physically harm other people. As Dr. King said, *"Nonviolence is a way of life for courageous people."*

Myth: Nonviolence works by "melting the heart of the oppressor".
Truth: While this has occurred, it is rare. More often, the nonviolent movement wields effective sanction power and forces the oppressor or opposition group to change a policy or surrender their position. We will be examining this later on in the study guide.

Myth: Nonviolence works because people are fundamentally good.
Truth: Regardless of our philosophic perspective on the inherent goodness or evilness of human beings, history seems to indicate that our species has the capacity for both extreme compassion and extreme cruelty. Nonviolent action works because the

movement matches the capacity of the opposition for waging struggle. Also, Gene Sharp posits that nonviolent action works because of the inherent stubbornness of human beings. We won't do what we are told to do, and we will do what we want to do - which can lead to mass noncooperation and nonviolent resistance. According to Sharp, nonviolent action works because human beings are fundamentally stubborn . . . and, given how prevalent human stubbornness is, I find this theory reassuring, don't you?

Myth: Nonviolence is a spiritual cult; you have to be a saint to use it.
Truth: History shows that nonviolent struggles have been primarily waged by ordinary people like you, me, and the family down the street. Many faith-based groups have been involved in organizing nonviolent struggles, but the majority of the participants in historical struggles are not saints, monks, or, in some cases, even regular church-goers.

Selma to Montgomery Marches, photo by Peter Pettus (Library of Congress) [Public domain], via Wikimedia Commons.

Myth: Nonviolence does not work against totalitarian regimes.
Truth: It does. These struggles often involve relatively higher casualty rates, violent repression, and different strategies than nonviolent struggles in more tolerant situations, but nonviolent action does work. Keep in mind that nonviolent action does not *always* work, but then again, violent means do not always work, either. And passive submission never works.

Myth: Nonviolence means your opponent won't use violence.
Truth: Almost all nonviolent struggles are met with some kind of violent repression. That's the bad news. The good news is that nonviolent action is uniquely equipped to deal with repression, minimize its effectiveness, and make the use of violence backfire on the opposition. You may also appreciate that the casualty rate is *significantly* lower for nonviolent struggles than for violent conflicts, which brings us to the next myth.

Myth: Nonviolence means we're all going to be brutally massacred without any way of defending ourselves!
Truth: As we just mentioned, the statistical likelihood of being killed in a nonviolent conflict is much lower than in a violent conflict for both participants and bystanders. Remember, in a violent conflict, the only option is for the two sides to shoot or attack each other. The likelihood of being harmed in such situations is much greater than if you had chosen to wage struggle with nonviolence. At the very least, you should be reassured that there is no such thing as "being killed by friendly fire" from participants in a nonviolent struggle. Bystanders may be harmed by the violent repression used by the movement's opposition, but the nonviolent movement itself does not wield

weapons, tear gas, rubber bullets, guns, etc., and cannot, therefore, harm bystanders. Through the course of this study guide, you will also learn that there are ways of avoiding the situation of being brutally massacred in the context of a nonviolent action. Wise strategies, for example, are the best way to preserve and protect the lives, liberties, and livelihoods of those involved in the struggle.

Myth: Nonviolence can only be used for good causes.
Truth: There is nothing about nonviolent action that makes it only work for good causes. Some terrible groups and individuals have used nonviolent actions quite effectively for very dubious purposes. As we will see later in the study guide, one of the types of repression that our opposition can use is a counter-nonviolent movement. And, at the end of the day, perhaps it is worth imagining a world where our conflicts are all waged using nonviolent methods, rather than violent.

Myth: Nonviolence is too slow; it takes lifetimes.
Truth: Empirical studies have shown that nonviolent struggles are not longer in duration than violent conflicts, particularly if achieving stated objectives is included in the analysis. In a variety of cases, nonviolent struggles have succeeded in as little as a few days.

For those who enjoy statistics, Erica Chenoweth offers the following information: For nonviolent anti-government campaigns, the average duration is 16 months. For nonviolent territorial (expelling a foreign invasion or ending an occupation) campaigns, it's 4.25 years. The average overall duration for nonviolent conflicts is about 2 years. This compares with over 6 years for violent anti-government campaigns and about 8 years for violent territorial campaigns (average overall for violent campaigns is about 7 years). Note: this is from the start to finish of contentious activity involving at least 1,000 participants and excludes the planning stages or lower-level contention of either violent or nonviolent conflicts.

Did you catch that? Nonviolent struggles take an average of two years, making them three times faster than violent conflicts for similar goals.

Myth: Nonviolent movements need to have a violent flank in order to succeed.
Truth: Violent flanks in predominantly nonviolent struggles actually *lower* the likelihood of success. This is due to some unique dynamics of nonviolent struggle that make it incompatible with violent methods. We will explore this more in Session Two.

Discussion Questions: Myths, Truth, and Your First Impression

- When you first heard the word "nonviolence", what came to mind?
- Over time, has your impression of nonviolent struggle changed?
- What were some of the myths and truths of nonviolent action that surprised

you?

- In *The Dandelion Insurrection*, what were some moments when the characters struggled with some of the myths about nonviolent action?
- In your own life, have you ever struggled with some of these myths? Which ones? What happened?

Conclusion: Nonviolent action is a powerful, potent force for change . . . especially when used strategically. Through the course of this study guide, we'll explore how to debunk the myths and live the reality of strategic nonviolent action!

Facilitators: Thank everyone for their reflections in this section. Next, we'll discuss the reasons people choose to use nonviolent action.

Discussion: Reasons for Choosing Nonviolent Action
(Time: 15mins)

Facilitators: In your own words, share with the group that people often have many reasons for choosing to use nonviolent action as the means to achieve social and political change. Some use nonviolent action because it is strategically sensible; others choose it because of moral or spiritual reasons. Motivations differ for each person, and it is often worthwhile to investigate these complex conversations. In this discussion, let's discuss *The Dandelion Insurrection* characters' motivations, and also our own!

Discussion Questions: Reasons and Motivations for Choosing Nonviolent Action

- Like people in real life, the characters in *The Dandelion Insurrection* have different reasons for adopting nonviolent methods as a form of struggle. What are some of the reasons the characters profess?
- What are some of the moral or strategic reasons for which you might consider using nonviolent methods in a struggle that you are involved in or to resolve an issue you care about?
- In *The Dandelion Insurrection*, Charlie's family expresses many viewpoints on what compels them to take action, or causes them to hold back. What are these viewpoints? What might your own family's viewpoints be, if you asked them to express their views on joining a nonviolent movement for change?
- What is a struggle you are involved in or considering joining? What compels you to take action on these issues? (Example: I am involved in the climate justice movement because I want humanity to continue existing on Earth. Or, I am involved in fighting poverty and income inequality because too many of my family - including myself - struggle with the problems caused by economic injustice.)
- Do you feel like nonviolent action may be the best way to address some issues that concern you? Why or why not?

"Make a wish, the dandelion says, and I will do my best to carry your seed-born hopes to fertile ground." - The Dandelion Insurrection

Luke Sekera-Flanders, photo by Nickie Sekera.

Session Conclusion:

In this session, we've explored myths and truths about nonviolent action, reasons people choose to use this style of resolving conflict, and shared our own personal stories. These elements are more interrelated than we might suspect at first, and as we journey further into studying how nonviolent action works, you may wish to return to these questions and see what has shifted in your thoughts.

Facilitators: This concludes our first session, getting to know one another, and establishing a common conversation. Thank your group for their insights and reflections. Next week, the group will be looking at the dynamics that make nonviolent struggle unique. Remind the group to read the next section. Thank everyone for their stories and reflections today. Make sure everyone knows where and when the next session will take place.

Closing: Facilitators, you may wish to close this session by reading the following quote and then inviting each person in the circle to add one or two words about what matters to their hearts.

"Everything mattered, not just the valley, but every nook and cranny of the earth; every stand of trees; every cluster of children in the school yard; each block of the teeming cities; every language that cried out on the tongues of immigrants; every joy, every sorrow; everything matters."

- The Dandelion Insurrection

Session Two: Dynamics of Nonviolent Struggle

"Remember, weapons never built a house, fed a child, or planted fields. We must turn to tools of nonviolence to build a chance for life." - The Dandelion Insurrection

Welcome back! Today's session is an introduction to the basic dynamics of how nonviolent struggle works to create change.

Facilitators: Welcome everyone and remind the group that we're going to talk about the basic dynamics of nonviolent struggle. Take a moment to say your name and perhaps a few words to describe how you're doing. For example, *"I'm Rivera and I'm excited for today's conversation."*

Discussion: Dynamics of Nonviolent Struggle
(Time: 1.5 hrs)

Facilitators: As with the Myths and Truths reading last week, let's go through the nine dynamics one at a time. Please encourage people in your group to summarize, in their own words, the dynamics as we go along. After each dynamic are a set of discussion questions. General discussion questions for this section follow at the end. To shake things up, there is also an exercise that accompanies Dynamic Six: Repression & the Aikido Effect.

Reading: Dynamics of Nonviolent Struggle

Nonviolent struggle follows unique dynamics, different than those of violent conflicts. By understanding these dynamics, we can plan wise strategies that increase the likelihood of success. There are many key elements to how nonviolent struggles operate and succeed, but in this study guide we will look at nine of them:

- Mass Participation
- Humanizing Effect
- Methods of Making Change
- Initiating vs. Reacting
- Duration and Escalation
- Repression and the Aikido Effect
- Maintaining Nonviolent Discipline
- Constructive and Obstructive Programs
- Stubbornness

A female demonstrator offers a flower to military police at an anti-Vietnam War protest. Arlington, Virginia, October 1967

Dynamic One: Mass Participation

Nonviolent struggles use widespread participation of the populace as part of their success. While some *actions* may succeed with smaller groups of participants, most nonviolent struggles seek to build *movements* that engage a broad group of people in a society. Nonviolent methods such as boycotts, strikes, and stay-at-homes become more likely to achieve their strategic goals when large amounts of people support and join in. While scholars of nonviolent struggle do not know exactly what percentage of popular participation in movements is required, they can observe that every movement that has actively engaged 3.5% of the population has succeeded. For context, 3.5% of the 300 million people in the United States would be 11 million citizens actively supporting the movement.

When a movement is broad-based, the opportunities for diverse nonviolent actions increase. For example, when historical nonviolent movements have included government bureaucrats, these individuals have engaged in slow-downs of government offices, misfiling or losing or delaying paperwork, and other forms of noncooperation. When a variety of workers are involved in nonviolent struggles, the possibilities for worker strikes and slow-downs emerges. When elders and youth participate, they bring different skill sets, energies, and capacities to the movement. The broader the participation, the more likely the nonviolent movement is to succeed.

Discussion Questions:

- What are some ways that the Dandelion Insurrection built mass participation?
- How did mass participation diversify the ways in which the Dandelion Insurrection was able to act?
- Who were some of the groups that joined the Dandelion Insurrection along the journey of the story? What skills and capacities did they bring with them?

Dynamic Two: The Humanizing Effect

"Nonviolence seeks to defeat injustice, not people." - Dr. Martin Luther King, Jr.

Unlike violence, which relies on dehumanizing the enemy, nonviolent struggle gains strategic and practical advantages by *humanizing* the opposition. This dynamic occurs for a number of reasons. Humanizing the opponent:

- **Cuts through the illusion of infallibility** of the opponent. (e.g. dictators)

- **Reduces the movement participants' fear** of the opponent.

- **Ensures that the opponent is held to the moral standards** of all human beings, rather than being exempted from decency because he/she/they are "monsters" or "sociopaths". This approach may help motivate citizens to take a stand against the tyranny of the opposition, since it is no longer acceptable behavior for any human being.

- **Creates awareness** in movement participants *and* the opposition that a "change of heart" is possible because humans (unlike evil monsters) change their hearts and minds all the time. This keeps the opportunities for change open, rather than limiting them.

- **Informs strategic understanding** more accurately, forcing movement strategists to take into account human, intangible factors such as emotions, psychology, shifts in perspective from the opposition group, and illogical or irrational responses from the opposition that are driven by other factors (paranoia, for example).

- **Helps maintain nonviolent discipline** because it circumvents the cultural training to "dehumanize an enemy and then attack him." When movement participants are trained to see their opposition as human beings, they may be less likely to fall into culturally habituated attack modes.

- **Reduces the likelihood of violent repression,** in some cases. The prime example of this dynamic lies in the relationship between protesters and the police. When protesters dehumanize police by calling them pigs, police are more likely to respond in the typical pattern of violence. In several places, nonviolent protesters have brought mirrors to demonstrations, holding them up so the police could see their own human faces. In these cases, the demonstrations remained nonviolent, or saw a reduction of violent repression.

- **Increases perception of opportunities** to erode the opposition group's pillars of support. One major challenge many movements face is seeing their opponent as monolithic. Humanizing the opposition trains the movement to perceive the opposition as human beings with complex motivations, reactions to the conflict, and approaches to resolving it. By identifying how these human beings

Carol Brown, Aug 2014. Photo by Dariel Garner.

create the opposition group's pillars of support, the movement can also identify strategic approaches to eroding or shifting that support to the movement or to a neutral stance.

- **Builds mass participation** in the movement because participants have exhibited high morality and a disciplined approach to the conflict, thereby impressing the neutral parties that the movement is reasonable and respectful.

The dynamic of humanizing also works for the nonviolent movement in strategic ways. When we humanize the movement, we build empathy, support, and understanding, and also increase the likelihood of activating the first and most important dynamic of nonviolent struggle: mass participation.

Additionally, sometimes the opposition is not expecting to be humanized by the movement. Accustomed to dealing with and operating through the classic pattern of *dehumanize and attack*, the opposition has a fully-prepared arsenal of techniques to manage the typical patterns of violent conflict. For example, let's say a student movement is seeking to end a dictatorship. If the students demonize the dictator, the dictator then feels justified in using his state-controlled media to tell the public that the students are punks without any respect for civil society. He will use arrests, beatings, tear gas, and violent means to disperse the student demonstrations and continue on with business as usual. But, if the students start from the position that the dictator (though known for brutal repression) is a human being who should sit down with the students and resolve the conflict peacefully, then they have demonstrated to society that their movement is reasonable, self-disciplined, respectful, and determined to resolve the conflict in a civilized manner. In so doing, they position the movement powerfully to aikido the repression of the opposition group.

Discussion Questions:

- How did the Dandelion Insurrection humanize or dehumanize their opposition?
- How did the Dandelion Insurrection humanize itself?
- At one point in *The Dandelion Insurrection*, Charlie chose to humanize the general public in an essay about people, not sheeple. How did this choice influence his ability to connect with the general public and move them into action?

"Reveal yourself as a human, not a statistic. Ask the police if they would beat your children if ordered . . . would they beat their own? We must remind them of their humanness. It is our only hope to stop the violence."

- The Dandelion Insurrection

Dynamic Three: Methods of Making Change
(or rather, Melting the Heart of the Oppressor . . . with a hot iron forge.)

One of the myths of nonviolent struggle is that it works by "melting the heart of the oppressor". While this sometimes occurs, studies of historical struggles demonstrate that there are several ways in which the opposition concedes to the demands of the movement.

Conversion, the opposition is converted to the cause of the movement.

Accommodation, the opposition accommodates some of the demands of the movement, but not all of them. Usually, the opposition maintains his or her position, and the system of power is not significantly altered.

Coercion, the movement successfully removes the ability of the opposition to control resources and erodes the opposition's pillars of support, thereby forcing the opposition into meeting the demands of the movement.

Disintegration, sometimes the movement is so successful in organizing noncooperation and defiance that the system of power collapses and the opposition does not even have sufficient power to surrender or yield concessions to the movement.

All four of these have occurred in real-life nonviolent struggles.

Discussion Question:

- In *The Dandelion Insurrection*, which of these dynamics seems to be unfolding at the end of the novel?

Bill Moyer, Backbone Campaign; Medea Benjamin and CodePink. Bush/Cheney Chain Gang in Dallas, Texas for the dedication of the Bush Lie-Bury, Arpil 2013.

Dynamic Four: Reacting vs. Initiating

Often, citizens move into action when faced with a crisis - a fracking company moves into town or a toxic waste disposal is being built near the schoolyard - but many powerful movements for social change do not only react to crises, they also initiate strategic campaigns and bring hidden problems to public attention by dramatizing the issue. Choosing to initiate campaigns leads to different options than simply reacting to the crises presented by your opposition. The more the movement plans, strategizes, and initiates the struggle, the more likely it is that the movement will hold the strategic advantage over their opposition, fighting the battle on their own terms.

Discussion Questions:

- What are some actions or campaigns in *The Dandelion Insurrection* that *reacted* to a crisis or a problem?
- What are some moments when the Dandelion Insurrection *initiated* a campaign or action to seize a strategic advantage?
- What are a few examples when the Dandelion Insurrection was faced with a crisis and crafted a strategy that not only met the crisis, but also powerfully advanced the movement?

Dynamic Five: Duration and Escalation

Nonviolent struggles sometimes appear to erupt spontaneously and quickly, but generally, these visible eruptions of resistance have years - if not decades - of build-up. In the Myths and Truths section, we mentioned that nonviolent struggles take an average of two years . . . once they reach the critical velocity of 1,000 participants. Think about a struggle you are involved in. Does it have that many people actively involved? The preparation for the major crux of the struggle may take some time.

For example, the Civil Rights Movement of the 1960's was preceded by several decades of other campaigns, including bus boycotts and attempts at desegregation. The height of the movement was a ten-year struggle, during which a major campaign was launched every year. Otpor, a Serbian student movement, succeeded in ousting dictator Slobadan Milosevic in two years, but it was preceded by many years of democratic movements that had not yet succeeded in getting rid of Milosevic, but may have laid the foundation for the breakthrough.

Nonviolent strategists often recommend planning for at least three years of struggle, developing campaigns that build cumulatively on each other during that time. This is called "escalation".

There are many ways of thinking about escalation in the context of a nonviolent struggle.

Stages of Escalation in a Nonviolent Campaign

- from the War Resisters International, *Handbook for Nonviolent Campaigns*

Stage of Escalation	Confrontational Action (actions that are directed against injustice in society)	Constructive Action (actions that help to construct a just order in society)	How it works
Stage 1: Bring the issue into the public arena	Protest (demonstrations, petitions, leaflets, vigils)	Presenting alternatives (teach-in lectures, show alternatives)	Publicizing to convince
Stage 2: Legal actions that deal with the issue	Legal non-cooperation (strikes, consumer boycotts, go slows)	Legal innovative activities (fair trade, free schools, alt. economic activity, ethical investments, nonviolent intervention)	Raising the stakes (costs) and minimizing the rewards for those committing injustice
Stage 3: Illegal actions that deal with the issue	Civil disobedience (sit-ins, blockades, tax resistance, strikes, war resistance).	Civil usurpation (sanctuary movements, pirate radio, reverse strikes, nonviolent intervention).	Redirecting power away from power-holders

Adapted and translated from German into English by Eric Bachman. This is a direct translation of the Chart of escalation of nonviolent actions on page 37 of Gewaltfreier Aufstand — Alternative zum Bürgerkrieg (Nonviolent Uprising — Alternatives to Civil War) by Theodor Ebert, Waldkircher Verlagsgesellschaft mbH.

Often, the escalation of a conflict is a dance between the groups waging the struggle. However, nonviolent movements can also plan to escalate a conflict as they grow the movement's capacity to wage struggle.

In one model (previous page), the first stage of a nonviolent campaign emphasizes bringing an issue to public attention using symbolic demonstrations, fliers, petitions, and constructive projects to draw attention to the issues and encourage change. If this does not achieve the desired result, the campaign may move to 'stage two'.

In the second stage, the campaign stages legal forms of nonviolent action that raise the costs for the opponent group. These may include methods such as strikes, boycotts, slow-downs, walkouts, etc. This may be sufficient for a movement to achieve its objectives, but if not, there is a third level of escalation.

The third stage of escalation uses nonviolent civil disobedience, noncooperation, and other nonviolent methods to force the opponent to yield to pressure and concede to the movement's demands.

Discussion Questions:

- Describe some moments of escalation in *The Dandelion Insurrection*. When did the opposition escalate the conflict?
- How did the Dandelion Insurrection escalate the conflict?
- In a struggle or issue you might be involved in, where and how do you see patterns of escalation occurring? Where do you think intentional escalation might help the movement?

"You can't lose if you never give up." - Gene Sharp, How To Start A Revolution

Dynamic Six: Repression and the Aikido Effect

Also referred to as *political jui-jitsu*, or *creating backfire*, the Aikido Effect refers to a unique dynamic that sometimes (but not always) occurs when violent repression is used on a nonviolent movement. If the movement maintains nonviolent discipline and perseveres with courageous, nonviolent action, the use of violent means of repression may backfire against their opponents. Instead of suppressing the movement, the repression may bring more neutral parties into actively supporting the movement, and sway former opposition group members to a more sympathetic stance to the movement.

"Civil resistance with mass participation never comes without serious repression."
- Erica Chenoweth, co-author of Why Civil Resistance Works

What Kinds of Repression Have Opponents Used?

- **Mischaracterizing** oppositionists as **criminals, "communists,"** terrorists, traitors, or coup plotters

- **Blaming foreigners and outsiders**

- **Co-opting oppositionists** by making legislative reforms

- **Paying off their inner entourage**

- **Counter-mobilizing** their own "nonviolent" supporters

- **Planting plain-clothes police as** *agents provocateurs*

- **Delegating repression to thugs,** hooligans, & paramilitaries

- **Use of terror** to scare people into submission

- **Censoring, spinning,** and using surveillance

- **Keeping out independent journalists**

- Using **pseudo-legitimate laws, practices, and debt burden** to reinforce their grip on power

- **Sharing information on how to suppress dissent** with allies

Note: This chart is used with permission from Erica Chenoweth. "Oppositionists" is what we might refer to as "the movement participants".

What is repression? Not all repression appears violent on the surface. Learning to recognize different types of repression prepares you and the movement for managing and dealing with them. Above is a chart that lists a few types of repression. Can you think of others?

Exercise: What is Violent Repression Meant to Achieve?

Materials: large sheet of paper or wipe-off board

Facilitators: Invite the participants to imagine what the Butcher, the Banker, the Candlestick Maker, and the illegitimate president hoped to achieve through using violent repression to stop the Dandelion Insurrection. Write these in one column on the left of a large sheet of paper. Some examples include obedience, fear, stopping the movement, and so on.

Next, explain that one way to manage violent repression is to invert the intended goals and do the opposite. Invite the participants to now list the opposite reactions to the expected goals of violent repression in a column on the right. (See example on next page.)

Example:

Through using violent repression the opposition hopes to achieve:	The movement can aikido the repression by doing the opposite of what it's intended to achieve:
fear	courage
obedience	continued disobedience
stopping the movement	continuing resistance and organizing

"Violence often achieves the opposite of what it intends to provoke. That opposite is the qualities of nonviolent struggle."

- Erica Chenoweth, co-author of Why Civil Resistance Works

Discussion Questions:

- What are some types of repression that were experienced by the characters in *The Dandelion Insurrection*?
- What were some approaches that the Dandelion Insurrection used to manage repression and overcome it?
- What were some moments where the Dandelion Insurrection aikido-ed the repression of the power elite, making it backfire on them?

"When fear is used to control us, love is how we rebel!"
- The Dandelion Insurrection

Banner at Occupy Eugene, 2011. Photo by David Geitgey Sierralupe.

Dynamic Seven: The Importance of Maintaining Nonviolent Discipline

A distinct dynamic of nonviolent struggle is that the movement must remain nonviolent as strictly as possible. Recent studies have demonstrated that when a nonviolent movement is accompanied by a violent flank, the rate of success in achieving their goals decreases. Around the time of the World Trade Organization Summits, a phrase came into North American activism, *diversity of tactics*. This refers to allowing both violent, nonviolent, and property damaging tactics to be used together in the context of a movement or particular event (such as the WTO protests). Many heated arguments arise around this phrase, but it is important to note that nonviolent struggles are undermined significantly by the presence of violent means.

This is due to a few factors. One, the unique dynamics of nonviolent struggle are, in fact, *unique*. Violent conflict operates differently. When violent means are included in a predominately nonviolent struggle, it undermines the effectiveness of the nonviolent dynamics. The primary dynamic of nonviolent struggle is mass participation. When violence enters the scene, participation decreases. Old ladies, young children, the physically weak, mothers supporting families, and many others cannot risk the almost certain dangers of engaging in a violent struggle. Nonviolence does not mean there will not be risks and casualties, but they tend to be significantly less, *and* nonviolent struggles provide a greater range of roles and ways of being involved in the struggle than violent conflicts.

Another reason you should treat nonviolence and violence like oil and water is because the Aikido Effect almost never occurs in the context of violent conflict. If anything, the opposite is more likely to happen. The public feels the opponent is justified (even if they do not agree with the opponent) in using violent force to defeat a movement that wields violent means. Police and military, in particular, tend to maintain obedience to the empowered class (often the opponent group) and not defect to the movement.

Discussion Questions:

- What were some moments in *The Dandelion Insurrection* when the movement struggled to maintain nonviolent discipline or ensure that the Dandelion Insurrection remained committed to nonviolence?
- How did the characters handle these situations?

"We have a right to hold a vegan potluck, and just because there is a diversity of food does not mean we have to eat your baloney." - Philippe Duhamel, on how to reply to proponents of a diversity of tactics.

Dynamic Eight: Constructive and Obstructive Programs

When we talk about nonviolent struggle, we often think of what Gandhi called *obstructive programs* that confront the opposition directly. However, Gandhi considered this to be just one branch of his work. The other - *constructive program* - is a way of carrying out a struggle through community-building and self-improvement by creating structures, systems, processes, and resources that are alternatives to oppression and promote self-sufficiency and unity in the resisting community. Gandhi considered constructive program to be equally important as the obstructive programs that resisted and undermined British control of India. The Salt March of 1930 is a classic case study of a campaign that combined the two to great effect. We'll look at constructive programs in more detail in Session Five.

Principles of Constructive Program:
(from the Metta Center for Nonviolence)

- Constructive Program is the scaffolding upon which the structure of a new society will be built while struggling against the old.
- By empowering the positive force of nonviolence, constructive work balances the "noncooperation with evil" with "cooperation with good", creating an unstoppable force.
- By providing the people with basic needs through their own work, the lie of dependency is proven wrong and the chains of oppression are shattered.
- It unifies diversity by creating work in which everyone can participate. Such work is ongoing, proactive, and builds community.
- Constructive program trains people to live a nonviolent life. Just as training for violent revolt means the use of military weapons; training for Satyagraha (Gandhi's word for nonviolent resistance, civil disobedience, and noncooperation) means constructive program.

Discussion Questions:

- What are some examples of constructive programs in *The Dandelion Insurrection*? How did these help build the "scaffolding of the new"?
- Conversely, what are some examples of obstructive programs with which the Dandelion Insurrectionists struggled against the destruction of the old system?
- How did constructive programs help the Dandelion Insurrection build participation and bring new people into the movement?
- Were there moments when the Dandelion Insurrection used both constructive and obstructive programs together? What were they? How did the two concepts support one another?

The SAPPER Squad from Vietnam Veterans Against the War.

"This country is ready to be reborn. Something fresh and new is fomenting in the fertile crumbling of the old!" - The Dandelion Insurrection

Dynamic Nine: Stubbornness As A Strength

We mentioned this dynamic briefly in the Myths and Truths section. Contrary to popular belief, the success of nonviolent struggle does not rely on the inherent goodness of human beings. Phew! Given our propensity for cruelty, injustice, and extreme acts of violence and oppression, it is probably a good thing that our "better nature" is not the driving success factor of nonviolence.

Nonviolent action scholar Gene Sharp posits that the success of nonviolent struggle relies on a less noble, but more plentiful, human characteristic: our inherent stubbornness. People will tend to do what they want to do, and refuse to do what they don't want to do. While this may be obnoxious in our two-year old children, it is a human trait that comes in handy when an invading army occupies your country or a dictator rises to power. Humans have great capacity for noncooperation. We also have tremendous ability to take courageous action when we perceive injustice and decide to take action to change the situation.

- What do you think about Gene Sharp's theory of stubbornness?
- Have you ever had a moment when you refused to do something you were told to do, and ended up waging a single-handed noncooperation campaign?
- Have you ever seen small children engage in the propensity for stubbornness and noncooperation?
- In many societies, including our own, the trait of individual stubbornness is trained into obedience. Do you think our culture is more or less obedient to authority? How is this trained? What does this mean for our current capacity to engage in nonviolent action, which is rooted in noncooperation with authority?
- Are there other human traits besides stubbornness that you feel are core to why nonviolent action might succeed? (For example, I personally suspect our propensity to love one another actually propels us into action, but that's just my theory.)

Discussion: Dynamics & Strategy

A nonviolent struggle is a dance. It moves, changes, and evolves over time. When we craft strategy for our movements, it is important to know that we are learning to dance with a partner (our opposition) who will grow, shift, and change. The dynamics of nonviolent struggle help us see the *ways* in which these changes might occur. Nonviolent struggle is not random. It follows trends and patterns that have been observed in one struggle after another. Each struggle is unique, of course, but their similarities offer useful insights into how a current struggle we are involved in might evolve.

In this discussion, let's look at how knowledge of the dynamics of nonviolent struggle may inform our strategic planning sessions.

Facilitators: Please note to the group that, in the upcoming sessions, we will dive more deeply into strategy for nonviolent struggles. In this section, however, let's take a moment to discuss the dynamics we've just explored and how they might influence us when we're planning an action or campaign.

Discussion Questions: Dynamics and Strategy

Facilitators: Invite the group to imagine they are part of the Dandelion Insurrection. Late one night, Zadie calls a group meeting via the Alternet, and proposes the concept of the Occupation of Greenback Street. Pretend that you are Charlie, Zadie, Inez, Aubrey, Lupe, Tucker, and other characters. Have one person in your group read the proposal:

"I propose a march to Greenback Street, followed by an occupation to force the elite to sit down with the Dandelion Insurrection and discuss our demands for real democracy, environmental sanity, restoration of civil liberties, and economic justice. Aubrey will issue an invitation to the elites to join him at his annual dinner. Unbeknownst to them, he will also invite the Dandelion Insurrection. I propose that we train the occupiers for several weeks in advance of the action, and prepare for repression from the police. What do you think?"

Next, discuss the following questions. Finding the "right" answer is not as important as exploring the way the dynamics of nonviolent struggle come into play when we're planning actions.

- Will the proposed march to Greenback St. and occupation build or decrease mass participation in the movement?
- How might this idea humanize or dehumanize the opposition? The movement?
- Is it likely that the opposition (the elite) will be moved into a position of change? Will they be converted to our cause through this action? Will they wish to accommodate some of our demands? If not, do we have the capacity to coerce them into agreeing to our demands? Is it possible that this action might disintegrate their system of power? Of these four possibilities, which are most likely? How might we increase the likelihood of success?
- Are we initiating change with this idea? Or are we reacting to a crisis? Are we likely to create a crisis (via repression) that the movement will be forced to react to? Are we initiating change that might create a crisis that our opposition must react to? Is this a good thing?
- Will this idea escalate our conflict in ways that we are prepared for? How will we maintain the energy it might generate? How long might this idea continue for? Can we hold an occupation on Greenback Street for as long as might be required? What do we do if we can't? (Note: this last question might

have been a good one for the fictional characters to ask *before* the occupation. In the book, Zadie considered it *during* the occupation - not the wisest strategy, but there you have it.)

- Is it likely to trigger repression? If so, is the movement prepared to manage the repression and possibly create an Aikido Effect?
- Does this action run any risks of weakening nonviolent discipline? If so, how can the Dandelion Insurrection prepare for that possibility?
- This idea is primarily obstructive in nature. Is there a constructive component that might be developed that would strengthen our capacity to do this?
- How might the innate stubbornness of human beings come into play among people in our movement? How might it come into play in our opposition? How might stubbornness (the propensity to not do what one is told and do what one wants) affect other members of the public?

Session Conclusion

Facilitators, after this discussion, thank all the participants for coming to the session. Remind them of the date, time, and location of the next session. Ask everyone to read the next section of the study guide in preparation for the next meeting. Next week, we'll be looking at basics of strategy for nonviolent actions, campaigns, and movements.

Closing: Ask the group to reflect briefly about the dynamics of nonviolent struggle. Did any of these dynamics surprise you? What is one dynamic that you will go home thinking about this week? At the end, you may wish to read this quote aloud:

"The Dandelion Insurrection is as small as baking bread in the oven and as large as bringing down dictators. It is practical and metaphorical, symbolic and literal. It was real. It was legend. It spread hope. It grew kindness. It sowed the seeds of resistance in the ground of adversity. Everywhere the concrete of control paved over the goodness of the heart, the Dandelion Insurrection sprang up through the cracks."
- The Dandelion Insurrection

Female delegates to the 1915 Women's Peace Conference in The Hague, aboard the MS Noordam. April 1915. Photo by Bain News Service, publisher [Public domain], via Wikimedia Commons.

Session Three: Movements - Campaigns - Actions!

"Strategy without tactics is the slowest route to victory; tactics without strategy is the noise before defeat." - Sun Tzu, the Art of War

Welcome! Today we're going to explore some elements of the three levels of nonviolent struggle: movements, campaigns, actions. (There is a fourth level, tactics, which we will examine later on in the study guide. For clarity and simplicity's sake, we'll stick with three levels for this moment. After we look at those, we'll discuss the role of establishing broad aims and objectives for a movement, and then finally, we'll explore the various methods of nonviolent action.

Facilitators: Welcome everyone. You may wish to do a quick check in with everyone. Let the group know that we're going to dive into some juicy material today. Ask if they had a chance to do the readings. Invite three people to review the definitions of movements, campaigns, and actions below. Then we'll proceed to the exercise.

"Planning without action is futile. Action without planning is fatal." - Philippe Duhamel

Reading: Grand Strategy, Campaign Strategy, and Action Strategy

Many of us are familiar with protesting on the street corner, or engaging in nonviolent actions. Yet, actions alone do not win a struggle. Using them strategically as part of a well-developed plan greatly increases the probability of success. Even in the context of a single campaign, rarely is one method of nonviolent action employed on its own. Gandhi's salt campaign, for example, combined civil disobedience, a symbolic march, speeches, pamphlet-ing, newspaper articles, economic noncooperation, and many other methods. Crafting wise strategy is key to employing the methods of nonviolent action in a manner that leads to the success of the movement. Nonviolent struggles have different levels of engagement and organization. And, since the details and content of strategic planning varies for those levels, it is helpful to think about how a nonviolent movement is constructed.

> **Movements** might identify a grand strategy - a general overview about how to achieve their aim(s).

> **Campaigns** are crafted as stepping-stones toward achieving the aim(s) of the movement. Campaign strategy is more limited in its scope, but sharper in its focus and attention to detail.

> **Actions** take place within the context of campaigns. Strategic planning for an action is limited to each occurrence and highly detailed. It may include

directions, where to meet, how long to hold the action, what to do if things go wrong, logistics of everything from sunscreen to legal aid in case of arrests, to witnesses if police repression is expected, and more. Action strategy is the most detailed of all three types of strategy.

Movements, campaigns, and actions each use differing levels of planning.

Grand Strategy: a plan of action or policy designed to achieve a major or overall aim of the movement.

Campaign Strategy: a more limited plan of action aimed at achieving a specific objective as part of a wider strategy.

Action or Tactic Strategy: a specific plan for an action or set of actions (called a tactic) within a campaign.

Bicycle ride & rally to stop artic drilling. Photo from Martine Zee

Exercise: Understanding the Difference (and relationship) Between Movements, Campaigns, and Actions.
(Time: 20mins)

Materials: large sheet of paper or wipe-off board
Facilitators: Draw a chart similar to the one below on a large sheet of paper or wipe-off board.

Movements	Campaigns	Actions

Movements	Campaigns	Actions
Civil Rights Movement		
Anti-Vietnam War Movement		
Suffrage Movement		
Labor Movement		
The Dandelion Insurrection		

people may suggest the Occupy Movement, which opens a great discussion later on about whether or not Occupy became a movement or a series of occupation campaigns throughout the United States.

Next, ask people to identify some campaigns that occurred as part of these movements. Start with the first one on your list, and write the campaigns in a column to the right of the movement.

Movements	Campaigns	Actions
Civil Rights Movement	Montgomery Bus Boycott	
	Nashville Sit-Ins	
	Mississippi Freedom Summer	
	Freedom Rides	

Next, ask participants to identify the tactics or actions that were used in some of those campaigns. Encourage them to refer to Appendix A: The 198 Methods of Nonviolent Action for reference. List some of the actions to the right of the campaigns.

Movements	Campaigns	Actions
Civil Rights Movement	Montgomery Bus Boycott	boycott
		speeches
		civil disobedience
	Nashville Sit-Ins	sit-ins
		boycott
		picketing
		march
		leafletting
The Dandelion Insurrection	Ending Martial Law	cazerolazo
		radio broadcasts
		articles
		stay-at-home
	The March to DC	march
		encampments
		offering sanctuary
		murmurations
		songs
		symbols
		defection of police

Conclusion: Facilitators, when you feel the group has grasped the concept, remind them that actions or tactics make up the nuts and bolts of campaigns. Campaigns are launched to address a limited objective within the context of a grand strategy to achieve the overall aims of the movement. Next, let's look at the broad aims and specific objectives that guide a movement.

"For life, liberty, and love!

Pour la vie, la liberté, et l'amour!"

–The Dandelion Insurrection

Reading: Aims and Objectives - Keep Your Eyes On The Prize

What shapes the strategic choices of a well-planned, organized movement? The aims and objectives. Often, when we are engaged in a movement for change, we conceive of our aim as *"stopping the problem"*. Yet, when we do that, we run the risk of missing the deep vision of our movement and the noble capacities of humans. For instance, I am involved in a campaign to *"stop fracking"*. But if I really think about it, I'm actually engaged in a movement to ensure clean air, water, and land for countless generations of human beings. Fracking is an obstacle to that aim. My efforts are rooted in a very profound concept of what it means to be a member of the human species here on planet Earth.

Establishing the larger scope of the movement is as important as identifying the smaller objectives. As you are working on this concept, remember that *campaigns* also have objectives. In general, campaigns and movements should share *broad aims.* (Otherwise, what are you working towards?) However, movements and campaigns may have different objectives. Movement objectives may be broader and more encompassing than specific campaign objectives, which are limited to the scope of the campaign, and perhaps include a higher level of detail and specificity.

- **Broad Aims** are the ideals or principles that the movement is attempting to achieve.
- **Specific Objectives** are the tangible, concrete goals through which the movement achieves the broad aims.

Exercise: Aims and Objectives for Movements
(Time: 15mins)

Facilitators: Invite your group to reflect on the differences between broad aims and specific objectives. On a flipchart or wipe-off board, draw a chart like the one below. Ask the group to name a movement and identify the broad aims of the movement. Next ask the group to list a few of the specific objectives that the movement worked on.

Movement	Broad Aims	Specific Objectives
Civil Rights Movement	Equality for All	Ending Segregation Gaining Voter Access Stopping Racism
Dandelion Insurrection	Life, Liberty, Love	Removing Hidden Dictatorship Ending Corporate-Political Collusion Stopping Environmental Destruction Repealing Unconstitutional Laws

Discussion: Facilitators, take 10-15 minutes and ask the group to discuss the difference between broad aims and specific objectives.

- What is the difference between movement aims and objectives?
- Why are they different?
- Why might it be important to identify the broad aims of the movement before or concurrently to establishing the specific objectives?
- Have you ever been involved in a struggle where establishing the broad aims of a movement changed or altered the specific objectives? (For instance, in my fracking campaign, a regulatory ordinance may have been a specific objective until the broad aim of establishing clean air, water, and land for all generations was stated. Then we knew that injecting toxic chemicals underground for all time would not suffice. We had to ban fracking completely to achieve our aim.)
- Are you involved in a movement now that could benefit from establishing clearer aims and objectives?

Conclusion: Facilitators, thank everyone for their thoughts. Broad aims and specific objectives guide the strategic planning at all three levels of nonviolent struggle: movement, campaign, and action. In the next section of the study guide, let's explore the specific methods of nonviolent action!

"I'm not going to keep scrambling to put out the government's fires. I want them chasing us because we're leading the revolution." - The Dandelion Insurrection

Methods of Nonviolent Action

In 1973, Gene Sharp identified the 198 Methods of Nonviolent Action. There are many more than one hundred and ninety-eight, several of which have been invented since Sharp wrote this list. Murmurations, for example, are a method invented for *The Dandelion Insurrection* that has not yet made it off the page and into the streets. In this section, we will familiarize ourselves with the methods of nonviolent struggle.

Exercise: Methods of Nonviolent Actions
(Time: 15 mins)

Materials: large sheet of paper or wipe-off board.

Facilitators: Share with the group that, in the novel, the Dandelion Insurrection used over eighty methods of nonviolent action. Invite everyone to turn to Appendix A: The 198 Methods of Nonviolent Action on page 97, and, running down the list of possibilities, name some of the methods of nonviolent action that appeared in *The Dandelion Insurrection*. As the participants name the method, write it down on one side of a large piece of paper or wipe-off board. On the other side, write down the specific example.

Method	Example from Dandelion Insurrection
Marches	The March to DC
General Strike	Widespread strikes at the end of the novel
Humorous Skits & Pranks	Flashing dandelion symbols on bare breasts

Hint: If the group needs prompting, ask them what methods were used during the evacuation, or in Rudy's town during martial law and the fracking invasion, or at Greenback Street.

Conclusion: As you can see, there are many methods of action available to a movement. In the next part of today's session, let's examine some characteristics that define these actions.

Reading: Characteristics of Nonviolent Actions

In the 198 Methods of Nonviolent Action, Gene Sharp uses six categories to describe the various methods:

- Protest and Persuasion
- Social Noncooperation
- Economic Noncooperation (Boycotts)
- Economic Noncooperation (Strikes)
- Political Noncooperation
- Nonviolent Intervention.

In addition, there are a few other ways of distinguishing, categorizing, or describing the various methods of nonviolent action. In this next section, we will explore:

- Symbolic and Non-Symbolic Nonviolent Actions
- Acts of Commission and Omission
- Concentration and Dispersion

Dandelion Banner at the People's Climate March, NYC, 2014, painted by Mona Caron. Photo by Margaret Flowers.

Symbolic & Non-Symbolic Nonviolent Actions

One important characteristic to understand is the difference between symbolic and non-symbolic actions. A *symbolic* action does not incur a direct cost or sanction upon the opposition. A *non-symbolic* action inflicts tangible economic, social, political or operational costs upon the opposition.

In general, acts of protest and persuasion (such as marches, vigils, rallies) are often primarily symbolic. This does not mean they have no effect, rather that the effect may be to sway hearts and minds, build participation in the movement, gain popular and widespread support, etc. However, the *costs* incurred by the opposition as a result of the action are intangible.

Acts of noncooperation (boycotts, strikes) and intervention (blockades, shut-downs), if successful, incur a tangible cost to the opposition. Sometimes this is economic: sales are lost, profits diminish, investors pull out. Other times the cost is operational: offices cannot function, supplies are not delivered, messages fail to reach their destination. There are also other ways of incurring tangible costs to the opposition, such as social ostracizing or expulsion from political, business, academic, or social clubs or institutions.

It is important to understand the difference between symbolic and non-symbolic actions. Millions of people can march around the cities in protest of an issue and the power holders can simply ignore them. But, when the millions of marchers blockade the offices of the power holders or encourage a boycott of a power holder's companies, the power holders must respond to the protestors in some way or risk incurring unacceptable costs.

Discussion: Symbolic and Non-Symbolic Actions
(Time: 10mins)

- What were some examples of symbolic actions in *The Dandelion Insurrection?*
- What were some examples of non-symbolic actions in *The Dandelion Insurrection?*
- In the Cazerolazo Countdown chapter, the banging of pots and pans is used to force the power holders to end martial law. Was this a symbolic or non-symbolic action?

Acts of Omission and Commission

"Everywhere, a resistance pushed back against the tide of destruction . . . Memos disappeared.
Uniforms weren't cleaned. Deliveries failed to show up.
'Total incompetence,' the authorities grumbled.
'Dandelion Insurrection', the people whispered."
- The Dandelion Insurrection

Acts of *omission* are when the person does not do a particular task or action that they normally would, such as when he or she stops working to engage in a strike. Paperwork that needs to be filed can be "lost" or delayed. Workers can simply not show up to do the work of the opposition, or they could claim to be completely booked for the season. The permutations are endless. In general, an act of omission occurs when the participants do not do a task or action that they normally would.

Acts of *commission* are when the person consciously engages in a task or action that he or she normally would not do, such as joining marches, rallies, occupations, or blockades. Acts of commission occur when the participants *do* something beyond their normal activities.

Why is this important? Sometimes, it is difficult to convince the populace to take action, particularly if the opposition uses repression frequently, or if the people are not socially used to engaging in nonviolent action. In such cases, less noticeable (though often equally effective) acts of omission become viable methods of waging struggle.

Discussion Questions: Acts of Omission and Commission
(Time: 10mins)

- What were some acts of omission that occurred in *The Dandelion Insurrection*?
- What were some acts of commission that happened?
- Were there times in *The Dandelion Insurrection* when choosing one type of action over another was more effective or more safe? What were those times? Why was an act of commission or omission more effective in those examples?

Dispersion & Concentration

Concentration and dispersion refer to methods that assemble human bodies in a physical space as opposed to dispersing those bodies over a widespread geographic area. This is important because when our physical bodies are congregated in an area (as for a march or rally or occupation) the casualties from violent repression could be high. When the movement chooses tactics that disperse people, such as a stay-at-home rather than a rally, then it is more difficult for the opposition to use violent repression against the movement participants. In situations where violence or other types of repression are likely to occur, strategists for nonviolent struggles must carefully analyze the objective(s) of the campaign or action, the projected benefits, and the overall costs to the movement. If the objectives can be achieved through an action that is less likely to result in costly repression to the movement, then a wise strategist uses the alternate action.

	Acts of Commission	Acts of Omission
Dispersion	flash mobs, overloading systems, cazerolazo (secondly least risky)	shut off, stay at home, strikes, boycotts (least risky)
Concentration	sit-in, occupations, march, blockades (most risky)	silence, go-slow, walk-outs (more risky)

A note from Rivera Sun: I adapted this chart (previous page) from Erica Chenoweth's presentation at the James Lawson Institute Aug 2014. Erica Chenoweth is the co-author of Why Civil Resistance Works, and a professor of conflict studies at University of Colorado, Denver.

In conclusion, the risk level of repression of various types of nonviolent actions can be summarized thus, from most risky to least risky:

1) Concentrated acts of commission (e.g. occupations)
2) Concentrated acts of omission (e.g. walk-outs)
3) Dispersed acts of commission (e.g. flash mobs)
4) Dispersed acts of omission (e.g. stay-at-homes)

Discussion Questions:
(Time: 10mins)

- What were some nonviolent actions in *The Dandelion Insurrection* that concentrated many people in a physical location?
- What were some nonviolent actions in *The Dandelion Insurrection* that were dispersed?
- During the Occupation of Greenback St., it became apparent that a violent crackdown from the police was imminent. Zadie made a strategic decision to disperse the occupation. What were the benefits of that choice? What were the drawbacks? Would you have chosen similarly or differently?
- The dynamics of concentration and dispersion also played out in the March to Washington DC. What happened from the moment Charlie and Zadie learned of the March's initiation to the conclusion of the March inside the nation's capitol? How did concentration and dispersion play strategic roles in assuring the success of the March?

"An idea shot through the three flanks like a bird in flight: Disperse, but move forward. The people vanished. All that remained was a rumble, an unease, a sense of tidal waves approaching."

- The Dandelion Insurrection

Session Conclusion

Becoming familiar with the 198 Methods of Nonviolent Action is a great source of inspiration and creativity for planning a campaign. Often times, we forget or overlook some amazing types of actions that could aid our struggle. Regularly revisiting the 198 Methods is a healthy exploration for anyone involved in strategic planning.

Facilitators, thank everyone for their participation and contributions today. Remind them of the date, time, and location of the next session. You may wish to give everyone a heads up: next week's session is action-packed and will take the full two hours. Come prepared and bring snacks. Ask everyone to read the next section this week. When we return, we'll be diving deeply into the tools of strategy for nonviolent campaigns.

Closing: Read the quote from Ellen Byrd in *The Dandelion Insurrection*. Go around and briefly say whether or not you agree with her. Are we fools? Are we armed with only justice, courage, and love? Or are we engaging in conflict with wisdom, strategy, and powers that lie outside the traditional power structure? What do you think?

"We are going into the battlefield armed with nothing but justice, courage, and committed love. Are we lunatics? Perhaps, but fools like us have shaped history more than once. It has been shown, time and again, that change wrought through nonviolent means endures far longer than the havoc of war and violence."
- The Dandelion Insurrection

Photo by Marirose Nightsong

"It is our love that calls us into action now – our respect for life and our compassion for creation require us to stand up to the forces that cause oppression, suffering, and destruction."
– The Dandelion Insurrection

Session Four: Strategic Analysis

"Inez persistently repeated the exact process through which tyrants crumbled, showing them the pillars of support that propped up the ruling elite, discussing how they could erode those like water and stone . . . " – The Dandelion Insurrection

Welcome back! This week, we'll examine how change is made, how to analyze a situation to see where to wage struggle and craft campaigns, and how to do strategic planning for a movement.

Facilitators: Welcome everyone. Check-in with the group and ask if any questions or thoughts emerged over the past week. Find out if anyone has specific questions they would like to explore today or in the weeks to come. Make a note, and if possible, try to make sure the group discusses those questions at some point. Let everyone know that we're going to do three exercises: Pillars of Support, Spectrum of Allies, and S.W.O.T.; but before that, we'll start with a discussion about how change occurs.

Discussion: Theories of Change
(Time: 15mins)

Facilitators: Ask one person from the group to read the quote below. Then we'll discuss the questions that follow.

"Theories of change are the ideas we have about how change happens in our communities, society, environment, and economics. They are the ideas we have about how we can get from the current situation we face, to realizing our visions and hopes of the future. We often assume that other people in our groups who have similar political beliefs have similar ideas and theories of change. However, in reality, there is often uncertainty, disagreement, and contradictions between people's ideas." – Jake Coleman, Handbook for Nonviolent Campaigns, War Resisters International

Discussion Questions:

- How do you think change happens? Is it "the guy at the top" who makes the decisions? Or is it people-power that forces change to happen? Is it a combination? Or something else entirely?
- Do you think it is necessary to "melt the heart of the oppressor" to see changes made?
- One theory of change is that government rules by the consent of the governed. Do you agree with this theory? Does everyone in the group agree or do some disagree?
- If the phrase "willing, coerced, uninformed or apathetic consent" was added would you agree with the theory that *governments rule by the willing, coerced, uninformed or apathetic consent of the governed?*

- Conversely, is it possible for governments to rule without the cooperation or consent of the governed?
- What about CEO's and owners of companies? College presidents and Boards of Directors? Parents of rebellious children?

Conclusion: Facilitators, remind the group that it is not necessary that we all agree. We are exploring ideas and considering concepts that may be different than our own. Encourage everyone to reflect on this discussion in the weeks to come. For now, we are going to move on to discussing a theory of change used in *The Dandelion Insurrection*.

Reading: Pillars of Support

The theory of change used in *The Dandelion Insurrection* follows an understanding outlined by Gene Sharp who posits that, although it can seem that a dictator or "guy at the top" has all the power, in actuality, he or she or a class of power holders relies on the cooperation and consent of others. Power holders require six categories of support to be able to hold their positions.

Authority, the belief among the people that the power holder is legitimate and that they have a moral duty to obey the power holder.

Human resources, the people who are obeying, cooperating, and providing assistance to the power holders. Note: both the number of people and their positions of importance are factors in this pillar of support.

Skills and knowledge, provided by the cooperating people, and needed by the power holders to accomplish tasks.

Intangible factors, psychological and ideological factors that may induce people to obey and assist the power holders.

Material resources, power holders must control of have access to property, natural resources, financial resources, the economic system, means of communication and transportation, etc.

Sanctions, the ability to threaten or apply punishments against the disobedient and noncooperative to ensure the submission and cooperation that are needed for the power holder to carry out his or her policies.

- adapted from Gene Sharp, From Dictatorship to Democracy

Without these resources, the power holder cannot order, control, manipulate, or force their will upon others. In other words, he or she cannot rule.

In our struggle, the opposition may not be a traditional ruler or power holder. It may be a group (like the police or a political party or a clique of bankers) or a business owner or board of directors or a social class. Using the term power holder also does not mean "power over us", but rather reflects that the person(s) hold power that we would like to see applied differently or removed from their control. We all have power, though some seem to have more than others. For the purposes of clarity, this study guide tends to use the term "opposition" to describe the people who oppose the interests of our movement. However, in this section on Pillars of Support, we will use the term power holder because we are examining the dynamics of how power is amassed, what it relies on, and how it can be eroded, removed, or disrupted.

"Resolve to serve no more and you are at once free. I do not ask that you place hands upon the tyrant to topple him over, but simply that you support him no longer; then you will behold him, like a great Colossus whose pedestal has been pulled away, fall of his own weight and break in pieces." – Étienne de La Boétie

Exercise: Pillars of Support
(Time: 20 mins)

Materials: a large sheet of paper & markers or a wipeoff board and pens

Facilitators: Using a large sheet of paper, draw a power holder on top of a pyramid. Ask the group: At the beginning of *The Dandelion Insurrection*, who are the perceived power holders? Is the general populace giving or withholding their consent? Are they cooperating or noncooperating with these power holders?

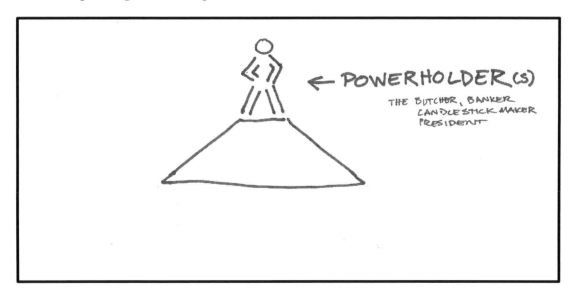

Draw a set of pillars beneath the pyramid. Start with six, and you can always add more.

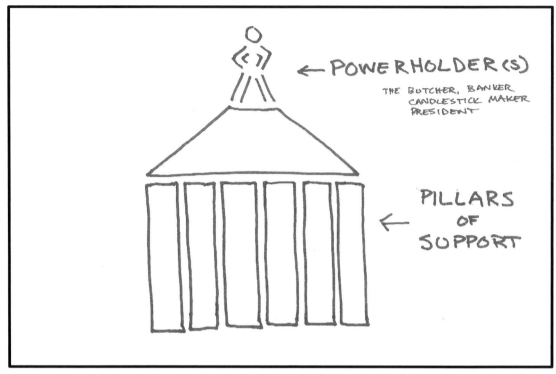

Power holders rely on "pillars of support" to stay in their positions. Ask the group: What resources (authority, human resources, skills and knowledge, material resources, intangible factors, and sanctions) do the power holders rely on? Write these on the pillars of support.

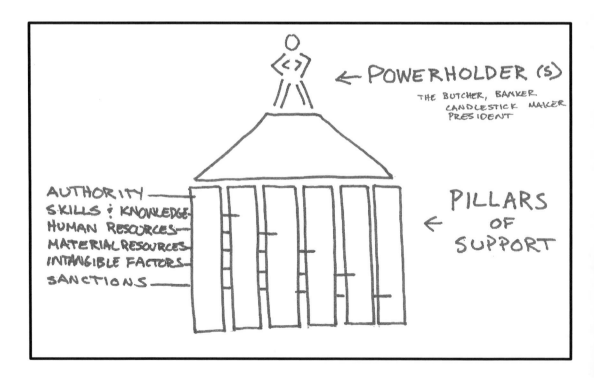

Ask the group, which groups or sectors of the populace provide these resources to the power holders? Write the exact services that are provided inside the pillars and the names of the people or groups who provide them underneath the pillars.

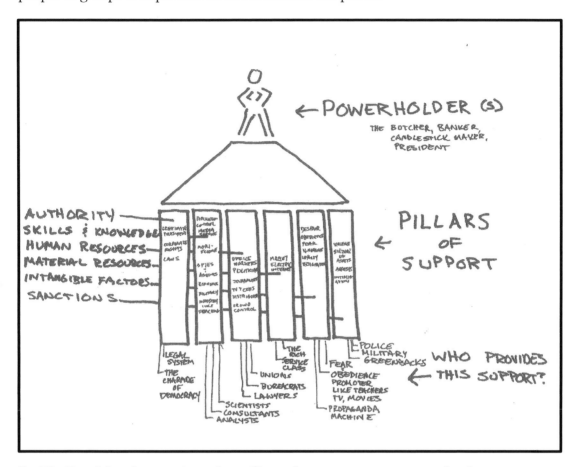

In *The Dandelion Insurrection*, what pillars of support were strongest for the power holders? What were the weakest?

Label each pillar on your diagram with one of the following:

> W : weak pillar
> S : strong pillar
> C : potential target for a campaign

(See the example on the next page.)

Note: A potential target for a campaign is an important distinction. Sometimes, a pillar is strong, yet it must be confronted and weakened by the movement. Other times, a pillar is too strong to be challenged by the movement at this moment. Also, a weak pillar may be a good target for a campaign, or it may be inconsequential at this time. The C label helps to identify pillars the movement should craft a campaign around.

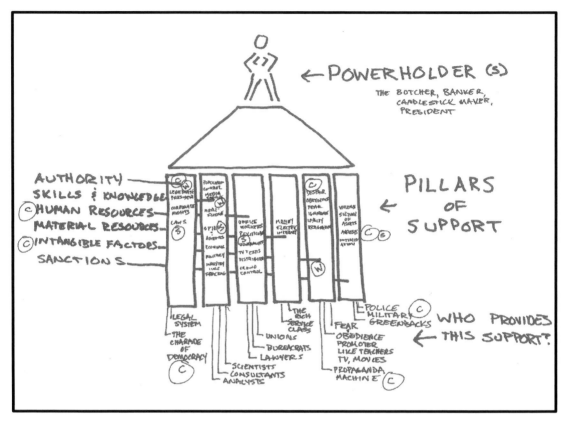

In your own words, explain that these are the pillars of support that prop up the power holders. In nonviolent struggle, the movement attempts to erode the pillars of support and shift supporting groups from a position of actively supporting the power holder to instead engaging in noncooperation, inaction, or active resistance to the power holders' rule. When

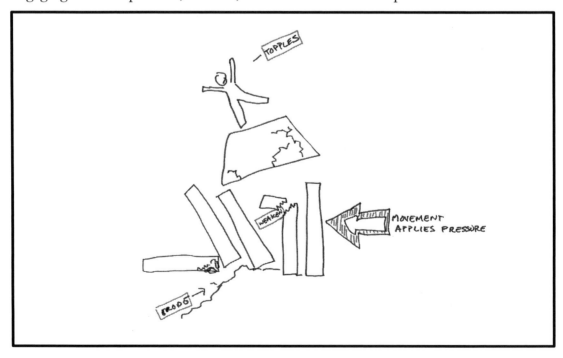

these supporting pillars disintegrate or switch sides, the power holder topples from his or her position.

Over the course of the book, how did the Dandelion Insurrection manage to cut off, erode, slow down or disrupt the power holders' ability to access support from these pillars? (Note to facilitator, you can prompt the group by inviting them to consider one category and/or sector of the populace. For instance, the sanctioning power offered by the police or military was a dynamic and changing factor in *The Dandelion Insurrection*. How did the availability and reliability of the police change during the course of the story?)

Ask the group how the following events shifted the Pillars of Support for the Butcher, the Banker, and the Candlestick Maker during the course of *The Dandelion Insurrection*.

- The Man From The North's articles being circulated and read.
- The evacuation from the cities.
- The Victory Gardens for the People project.
- The Greenback Street Occupation and subsequent murmurations.
- The witch hunt for Zadie Byrd Gray.
- The unleashing of the Alternet.

Conclusion: The Pillars of Support exercise is a classic tool of nonviolent strategists. By understanding the strengths and weaknesses of our opposition, we can begin to see where our struggle should be waged and how. In the next exercise, the Spectrum of Allies, we will look at the *people* in our situation and map them on a spectrum from active opposition to active supporters.

Swarm Orlando to Save the Bees, Aug 2014, photo by Rich Hillwig.

Exercise: Spectrum of Allies
(Time: 20mins)

Materials: A flipchart of paper or a wipe-off board, markers.

Another way of analyzing the strength of the opposition and the movement is to look at the "Spectrum of Allies". Every person, group, institution, or sector of the populace will fall somewhere on this spectrum. Nonviolent struggle seeks to shift active opponents into neutral parties and neutral parties into active supporters.

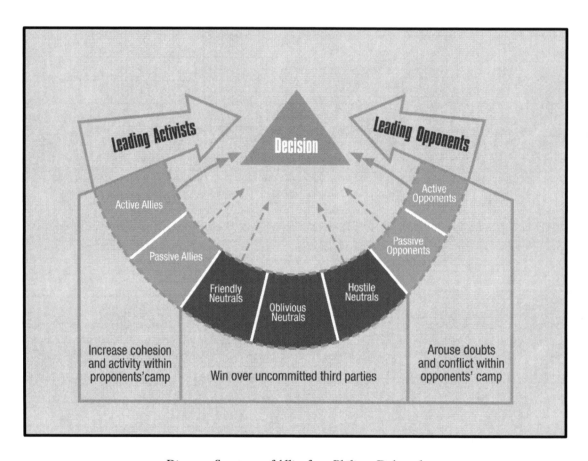

Diagram: Spectrum of Allies from Philippe Duhamel

Facilitators: Draw a line on a large flipchart. On the left, write "active supporters of the movement". On the right, write "active opponents of the movement." In the middle, write "neutral". Add two more categories to the left, "passive allies", "friendly neutrals". Add two categories to the right, "hostile neutrals" and "passive opponents". Your line should look like the diagram on the next page.

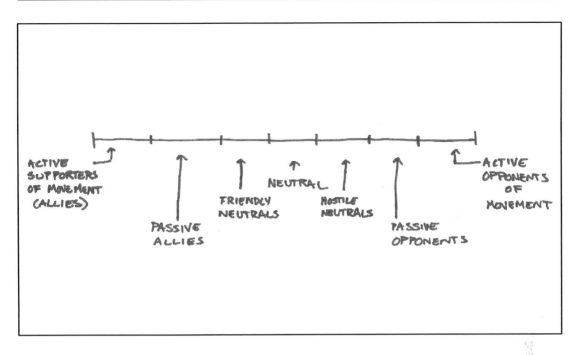

Next, let's map a Spectrum of Allies, using *The Dandelion Insurrection* as an example.

Ask the group to name some influential groups of people in *The Dandelion Insurrection*, and where they stood on the Spectrum of Allies at the start of the novel. Consider the police, the military, the general populace, the Suburban Renaissance, Charlie's family, Zadie's parents, the people in Tucker's town, the Butcher, the Banker, the Candlestick Maker, the President. Write their names on the spectrum.

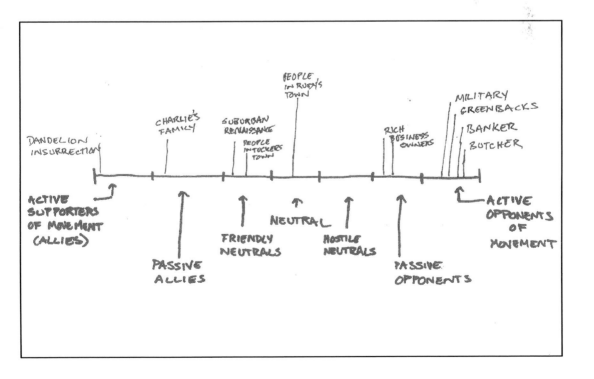

By the end of the novel, which of these people, groups, institutions, or sectors of the populace had shifted their positions? Draw a set of arrows indicating those shifts.

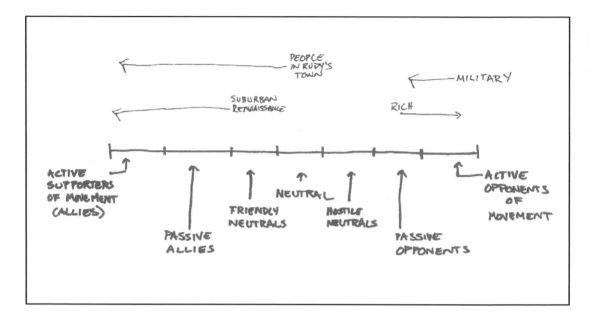

Strategic campaigns will cause advantageous shifts on this Spectrum of Allies. Consider a few campaigns in *The Dandelion Insurrection*. How did the people, groups, institutions, or sectors of the populace move along the Spectrum of Allies during the martial law and cazerolazo, the evacuations, the witchhunt for Zadie, the March, the Occupation of Greenback St., etc.?

Shifting a group along the Spectrum of Allies is a common objective of a nonviolent campaign. Look at the Spectrum of Allies at the start of *The Dandelion Insurrection*. What groups were good potential targets for a campaign to shift them? Mark these with a C. (We will use this in the final exercise of this session.)

Were there any groups that did not shift on the Spectrum? As a group, choose one group and brainstorm a fictional campaign by which *The Dandelion Insurrection* could have shifted that group.

Conclusion: The Spectrum of Allies exercise is a good way to map the terrain of people in relation to your movement. Next, we will look at an exercise that helps us examine the dynamic relationship between the movement and the opposition.

Facilitators: This is a good time for a quick, five minute break. Strategic analysis exercises can be intensely analytical, so invite the group to shake out their bodies, get a drink of water, use the restroom, have a snack, and so on. Let them know that when we return from our short break, we'll be looking at the relationship between the movement and the opposition.

Exercise: Assessing the Movement & the Opposition - S.W.O.T.
(Time: 20mins)

Materials: A flipchart of paper or a wipe-off board, markers.

S.W.O.T. stands for: Strengths, Weaknesses, Opportunities, Threats. The analysis model offers a way to analyze both your movement and the opposition.

Facilitators: For this exercise, break the group into two smaller groups. Again, we will use *The Dandelion Insurrection* as the example. One group will do this exercise for the opposition. The other group will do the exercise for the Dandelion Insurrection.

Each group needs a large piece of paper. At the top, write the name of the group you are analyzing (Hidden Dictatorship or Dandelion Insurrection). Draw a diagram like this:

Strengths	Weaknesses
Opportunities	Threats

Take five minutes and write down the strengths of your group. For the opposition, this may look like:

Strengths: Control of government, money, authority, police and military sanction power (etc.)	Weaknesses
Opportunities	Threats

Take five minutes to write down the weaknesses. For the Dandelion Insurrection, this may look like:

Strengths	Weaknesses
	lack of traditional leadership command, vulnerable to state persecution, no traditional authority, lacking resources of money, except for small gardens the DI is reliant on the opposition's systems for basic needs.
Opportunities	**Threats**

Next, take five minutes to identify some opportunities available for your group. Did the hidden dictatorship have an opportunity to catch Charlie and Zadie? Did the Dandelion Insurrection have an opportunity to erode a pillar of support for the hidden dictatorship? List these.

Finally, take five minutes to identify the threats to your group. Start right off with your group's opposition. (For example, the Dandelion Insurrection as a movement is a threat to the Hidden Dictatorship.) Remember, an opportunity for the opposing group is often a threat to your group. The hidden dictatorship's capacity to catch Charlie and Zadie is a threat to the Dandelion Insurrection.

Come back together as one whole group. Bring your charts. Take turns sharing your S.W.O.T. analysis with members of the other group. Did the opposite group identify some elements about your own group that you didn't?

Looking at the charts, ask each group to identify potential targets for campaigns. Take a marker and write C - DI for a potential campaign for the Dandelion Insurrection. Use the initials C - HD for a campaign for the Hidden Dictatorship. Your marks will end up on both flipcharts. What have you discovered through this process?

Conclusion: The S.W.O.T. exercise helps us understand the dynamic relationship between our movement and the opposition. Next, we will combine the Pillars of Support, Spectrum of Allies, and S.W.O.T. to help identify campaigns.

Exercise: Putting It All Together - Pillars of Support, S.W.O.T., Spectrum of Allies & Identifying Potential Campaigns

(Time: 10 mins)

Materials: A flipchart of paper or a wipe-off board, markers.

Facilitators: Spread out all the charts from today on the floor or tape them to a wall (use painter's tape so you don't pull off the paint. A friend of mine once ripped the gold gilt off a hotel conference room trim by taping up his paper charts with the wrong kind of tape).

On the charts, look for all the C's that mark the potential campaigns (except for the C-HD's in the last exercise). On a clean sheet of paper, make a list of these. The list will include campaigns that revolve around:

- Strengthening a weakness in the movement
- Eroding or removing a pillar of support for the opposition
- Shifting a group of people toward the movement's side of the Spectrum of Allies
- Achieving a stated objective of the movement
- Grasping an opportunity
- Protecting the movement from a potential threat

Facilitators: Thank everyone for this amazing list! Let them know that we will be using this list next week in our session on planning cumulative campaigns!

American Civil Rights Movement, March on Washington (public domain)

August 28, 1963

Session Conclusion

Using these exercises, you can identify strategic campaigns for your movement. In the next session, you will learn how to examine potential campaigns and design a cumulative series of campaigns.

Facilitators: Thank the group for their hard work today! You may wish to check in with the group and ask them to share reflections on today's experience. Remind them of the date, time, and location of the next session. Ask the group to please read the next section.

Closing: Read the quote below. Then, ask each person to reflect on the exercises we just completed. Would they use them in the context of a real life struggle they were involved in? Why? How?

"Charlie had spent months researching the article that outlined the overarching strategy of the Dandelion Insurrection, critiquing it rigorously before distributing it. It wasn't rocket science, Charlie shrugged to himself, but it wasn't a cakewalk, either!"

– *The Dandelion Insurrection*

"Nonviolence is not something that is done to someone. It is something that is done with someone." – *anonymous.*

Session Five: Crafting Cumulative Campaigns

"Nonviolence is the worst form of conflict management - except for all the rest."
- Tom H. Hastings, adapting Winston Churchill.

Welcome back! This session will focus on planning cumulative campaigns and actions. Ideally, campaigns build cumulatively upon the strategic advances of the previous campaigns. All too often, we see a series of nonviolent actions following a random series that preceded it. Using the knowledge we gained through strategic analysis exercises like Pillars of Support and Spectrum of Allies, we can plan a series of campaigns that build cumulatively on the previous campaign's success.

Facilitators: Welcome the group. Ask them to go around and share any reflections from last week's session. Let them know that today we're going to focus on campaigns, the stepping stones of movements. We are also going to look at constructive programs as a particular kind of campaign that deserves some focus and attention. As a review of this week's readings, and to start today's session off, ask a few participants in the group to say in their own words what each of the four points (strategic analysis, broad aims, specific objectives, and grand strategy) means.

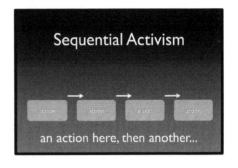

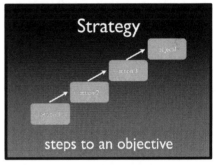

Images courtesy of Philippe Duhamel.

Reading: A General Review

In Session Three, we outlined the different types of strategy for the three levels of nonviolent struggles: movements, campaigns, and actions. To refresh our memories:

Movements identify a grand strategy - a general overview about how to achieve their aim(s).

Campaigns are crafted as stepping-stones toward achieving the aim(s) of the movement. Campaign strategy is more limited in its scope, but sharper in its focus and attention to detail.

Actions take place within the context of campaigns. Strategic planning for an action is limited to each occurrence and highly detailed. It may include directions, where to meet, how long to hold the action, what to do if things go wrong, logistics of everything from sunscreen to legal aid in case of arrests, to witnesses if police repression is expected. Action strategy is the most detailed of all three types of strategy.

In today's session, we will examine how the following four concepts inform the building of a cumulative series of campaigns:

- Identifying the **broad aims** of the movement
- Establishing **specific objectives** the movement wishes to achieve
- Working on a **strategic analysis**
- Developing a **Grand Strategy**

Let's look at each of those.

Broad Aims are the ideals or principles that the movement is attempting to achieve. The broad aims of the Dandelion Insurrection might include: democracy, safety, economic justice, environmental protections, civil liberties, a culture of respect for humanity. (Life, liberty, and love!)

Specific Objectives are the tangible, concrete goals through which the movement achieves the broad aims. The specific objectives of the Dandelion Insurrection are more tangible and defined than the broad aims. Whereas the broad aims of a movement generally remain the same, the specific objectives may shift according to their strategic importance for the movement. For example, the Dandelion Insurrection began with a few specific objectives: expose and remove the hidden dictatorship, end mass surveillance, restore civil liberties (particularly the right to speak and assemble), stop environmental destruction. But along the way, the movement was forced to add some objectives: end martial law, prevent mass incarceration, halt the persecution of Zadie and Charlie, establish a secure communications platform.

David Gibson, organizer.

Remember, both *movements* and *campaigns* can have specific objectives. In Session Four, we identified that campaigns might revolve around the specific objectives of:

- Strengthening a weakness in the movement

- Eroding or removing a pillar of support for the opposition
- Shifting a group of people toward the movement's side of the Spectrum of Allies
- Achieving a stated objective of the movement
- Grasping an opportunity
- Protecting the movement from a potential threat

Grand Strategy is a plan of action or policy designed to achieve a major or overall aim of the movement. The Grand Strategy of the Dandelion Insurrection might read something like: Get rid of the hidden dictatorship by using nonviolent action to weaken the hidden dictatorship's power. Grow a pro-democracy people's movement to replace it and represent the people.

Grand Strategy is not concerned with the crises that arise in the course of the struggle (evacuations, martial law, beatings, mass arrests, trials in absentia). Grand Strategy has its eyes on the prize and is lashed to the tiller of the ship. Grand Strategy doesn't break it down for Charlie and Zadie, Inez, Lupe, Tucker and Tansy. It stays firm as the North Star and guides the movement. Only rarely will a well-crafted Grand Strategy need to be revised. For instance, if the hidden dictatorship dissolved into a multi-party factional dispute for control of a democratically-elected Congress, then the Dandelion Insurrection movement might drop the first part of the Grand Strategy (get rid of the dictatorship) and continue with the second (grow a pro-democracy people's movement to represent the people).

So, how do we turn a Grand Strategy into a workable plan for achieving our goals? Through conducting a thorough strategic analysis and identifying specific objectives and campaigns.

Love-In-Action Taos demonstrating on the Taos Plaza, Taos, NM, Aug 2104.

Photo by Bill Moeller.

A **Strategic Analysis** is a thorough examination of the strengths and weaknesses of both the movement and the opposition, as well as the social-political terrain or context in which the struggle is being waged. A Strategic Analysis was not part of the Dandelion Insurrection's story . . . if it had been, the characters might have avoided a lot of trouble! In this study guide, however, we have engaged in many components of developing a strategic analysis by looking at: the Pillars of Support; the Spectrum of Allies; S.W.O.T. (Strengths, Weaknesses, Opportunity, Threats); and identifying potential campaigns. On top of that, a thorough strategic analysis might include an even deeper examination of the movement, the opposition, and the general public, resources, geography and terrain, political climate internationally as well as nationally, and other factors.

(Note: Appendix B: Outline of a Strategic Planning Process on page 103 offers a format for taking a group through a strategic planning session.)

The overwhelming amount of detail found in the strategic analysis informs the identifying of campaigns and the development of a cumulative series of campaigns to achieve the objectives, broad aims, and grand strategy of the movement.

Exercise: Crafting Cumulative Campaigns - the Stepping Stones of Movements
(Time: 30mins)

Materials: A flipchart of paper or a wipe-off board, markers, and the sheet of paper that has the list of campaigns from last week. Participants will need notebooks and pens.

Facilitators: Bring out the sheet of paper that has the list of campaigns from last week. Ask people to pair up or form small groups. Each group will focus on a single campaign from the list. These may be campaigns that were described in *The Dandelion Insurrection* or they may be imaginary campaigns.

Give each group several large sheets of paper. Ask each group to draw a large table on their paper. Each group will fill out the following information on their campaign:

- Broad Aims of the movement that the campaign seeks to achieve.
- Specific Objectives of the campaign.
- Methods of Nonviolent Action that might achieve those objectives (in combination or on their own).
- Duration & Timing
- Participants in the campaign
- Targets of the campaign*
- Shifts in the Spectrum of Allies

- Required Resources & Costs to the Movement
- Potential Risks to the Movement
- Movement Advantages if campaign succeeds
- Final Analysis: Are the potential advantages worth the costs and risks?

* Targets of a campaign may be different than the opposition of a movement. The *target* may be a potential ally that the campaign seeks to move into action. Or the target may be a particular material resource that the movement seeks to deny the opposition. Or the target may be the opposition itself. It depends on the objectives of the campaign.

Below is an example from the Cazerolazo Campaign to End Martial Law:

Name of Campaign	Broad Aims	Specific Objectives of the Campaign	Methods	Duration & Timing
Cazerolazo	Civil Liberties, Safety from Repression & Restoration of Civil Law	Ending Martial Law, Noncooperation with injustice, Remove legal justification for military's support of corporate frackers.	stay-at-home, pots & pans protest, radio broadcasts, articles, noncooperation, civil disobedience	**Duration:** Until martial law is repealed. (Exact duration unknown) **Timing:** Begin at set time, en mass.

Name of Campaign	Participants in the campaign	Target(s) of the campaign	Spectrum of Allies shifts
Cazerolazo	General populace, as many as possible. Organizations and groups, such as churches, social clubs, neighborhood associations, action groups, and academic institutions.	**Primary:** President **Secondary:** Social and Political Power Class; Military	**New Active Supporters:** General Populace, Churches **Passive & Active Opponents Shifted to Active Supporters of Campaign Objective of Ending Martial Law:** President's Wife, Social and Political Power Class, Military

Name of Campaign	Required Resources /Costs	Potential Risks	Movement Advantages if campaign is successful	Are the potential advantages worth the costs and risks?
Cazerolazo	Mass participation of populace, printed copies of articles, legal fees for those potentially arrested during the campaign, medical care for anyone met with violent repression.	Heavy violent repression via the military; mass arrests; inability to sustain unity and duration; failure of campaign would undermine DI's credibility; low participation would make participants vulnerable to opposition's repression; opposition could stop the spread of the cazerolazo.	End martial law, restore civil liberties, build participation in Dandelion Insurrection, erode military support of corporate-political state, demonstrate power of the people to the populace, break through fears of populace.	Yes.

Next, have each pair or group consider the following questions and take notes:

- Does this campaign require resources that the movement does not have? If so, what are they?
- What risks could cause the campaign to fail? What are those risks? How could the movement mitigate them?
- Does this campaign involve costs that are too high for the movement to bear? If so, what are they?
- How difficult is it to reach the primary target of the campaign through the nonviolent actions chosen? Are there ways to impact the primary target more powerfully and effectively? What might those be?

Conclusion: Facilitators, reconvene the whole group. Give each pair or group a set amount of time (2-3 mins) to explain their campaign broadly. Then, let everyone know that now we're going to explore how this information about the campaigns can aid us in crafting a cumulative campaign strategy.

Exercise: Ordering Cumulative Campaigns
(Time: 10mins)

Facilitators: Ask the whole group to stand in a line, holding one of the charts from the previous exericise that has the information about their campaign on it.

Share with the group that, right now, they are standing in a chronology of campaigns from left to right. (The facilitator's left to right.) Unfortunately, this is what a movement without any strategic planning looks like. The campaigns are launched in any order without careful consideration of the sequence. For example, first, the movement works on ending martial law. Then, for no apparent reason, the movement switches to fighting fracking. After that, the movement decides to start planting Victory Gardens. (You get the idea?)

Next, let the group know that we're going to attempt to arrange the campaigns in a cumulative sequence using the following questions and moving people around in the line. In order, ask the following questions:

- Does anyone's campaign require a major resource that the movement does not have? What?
- Does anyone's campaign supply that resource as one of the advantages of their campaign? If so, then stand to the left (facilitator's left) of the other campaign to indicate that your campaign should precede the other.
- Does anyone's campaign have a specific timing or duration? Does anyone else need to come before or after that timing? Move to the left or the right accordingly.
- Does anyone have a campaign that needs mass participation and could benefit from several movement-building campaigns preceding it? (Stand to the

right.)

- Does anyone's campaign build mass participation? (Stand to the left.)
- Does anyone's campaign threaten mass participation? Okay, so let's not have that campaign immediately precede the campaign that requires all those people. Let's put it after or way before that mass participation-requiring campaign.
- Does anyone have a campaign that strengthens the movement? And does anyone have a campaign that may incur heavy costs to the movement? Could the strengthening campaign serve as a rebuilding campaign? Or is it better suited to preparing the movement for the costly campaign? Move accordingly.
- Does anyone's campaign shift an ally into action or neutralize an opponent? Does anyone's campaign need those shifts to occur before their campaign launches? Move accordingly.
- What other considerations should we look at as we work on order of campaigns? Do we have a campaign that opens up an opportunity that another campaign focuses on? Does one campaign eliminate a potential threat to the movement that resolves the focus of another campaign? Do we need to leave a blank space in front of a campaign to indicate that another campaign should precede it?

Facilitators: Keep asking questions and moving the campaigns around until participants grasp the idea. Then, write down the final order in the format of a staircase. Leave blank stairs for any place that feels like it needs a campaign to prepare the movement to wage the next campaign in line. Remind the group that strategy is dynamic. As the situation alters (as it should, if your campaign is well-organized), you will need to adjust your plans to account for that.

Conclusion: Crafting a cumulative campaign strategy requires identifying the potential campaigns, their required resources, potential risks, and costs to the movement; and then comparing those campaigns to find a logical sequence of action.

Facilitators: This is a good moment for a short break. Give participants 5-10 mins to shake out their legs, clean up the sheets of paper, and use the restroom. When we reconvene, we'll be switching gears to examine a very special and powerful type of campaign: the constructive program!

Rivera Sun's favorite constructive program: local agriculture. Photo by Dariel Garner.

Reading: Constructive Programs

"The Suburban Renaissance pooled the resources of its troubled communities, offering childcare, carpools, and community gardens as a strategy for mitigating the expensive effects of isolation. The 'largest subversion of the dominant paradigm in American history' turned out to be something as ordinary as apple pie . . . people helping people."
– The Dandelion Insurrection

An often-overlooked element of social movements is the role that constructive programs play in strengthening the movement, building the new systems, and undermining the power of the opposition.

"Constructive Program"
(from the Metta Center for Nonviolence)

Constructive program is a term coined by Gandhi. It describes nonviolent action taken within a community to build structures, systems, processes or resources that are positive alternatives to oppression. It can be seen as self-improvement of both community and individual. Constructive program often works alongside obstructive program, or civil disobedience, which usually involves direct confrontation to, or non-co-operation with, oppression. Constructive program is doing what one can to imaginatively and positively create justice within one's own community.

Gandhi at the spinning wheel, late 1920s, India. (public domain image)

Confrontations — whether violent or nonviolent — can capture attention, intrigue the media, and catalyze fledgling movements. However, by themselves even poignant instances of nonviolent resistance cannot build or sustain movements. Gandhi understood that Constructive Program, at its core a positive principle, would draw many people to a program of principled nonviolence. Moreover, there is a special power and directness in improving oneself and one's community rather than, or alongside, trying to change an oppressive system.

Gandhi defined Constructive Program quite early in his career and coined the term to denote the myriad of activities that he felt were prerequisite to carrying out the more overt and confrontational modes of nonviolent action. For example, he established four ashrams in the course of his long career where satyagrahis, nonviolent actors, could live a nonviolent, creative life that was largely self-sufficient and sustainable. As Constructive Program took on more and more importance over the course of the Indian freedom struggle, the charkha or spinning wheel became its symbol. By using the spinning wheel to create home-spun cloth, each Indian could participate in the struggle to build a sustainable economy separate from the British textile industry. Spinning enabled every Indian to engage in the 'bread labour' of fulfilling a basic need, gave employment to millions of idled workers, *and* allowed all Indians to participate directly in freeing India from England's economic domination. The spinning wheel became the 'sun' in the 'solar system' of many other projects.

Many modern nonviolent movements pay little or no attention to Constructive Program. Instead they focus all of their energy on non-cooperation and civil disobedience. Activists are tempted to reason that they can build a new society after the present regime is gone. Gandhi argued that the reality was reversed, and that the chances for permanent change were less without Constructive Program. Recent events seem to bear this out. While nonviolent insurrectionary movements in the second half of the 20th century have successfully liberated people from repressive regimes in South Africa, the Philippines, Poland, the Czech Republic, Serbia, and many other places, in almost all cases the same problems of poverty and other forms of structural violence have returned to undermine the gains of the nonviolent program. This is not because nonviolence doesn't work but because nonviolence without Constructive Program is incomplete.

Gandhi picking up grains of salt. April 5, 1930, public domain, via Wikimedia Commons.

Key Aspects of Constructive Program:

- projects should not be merely positive but have political and social significance,
- they should be empowering to all participants,
- ideally, they should be non-symbolic (or be concrete projects with symbolic value), and finally,
- they should have revolutionary potential, even when they are as far as possible not *directly* confrontational.

Principles of Constructive Program:

- Constructive Program is the scaffolding upon which the structure of a new society will be built while struggling against the old.
- By empowering the positive force of nonviolence, constructive work

balances the "noncooperation with evil" with "cooperation with good", creating an unstoppable force.

- By providing the people with basic needs through their own work, the lie of dependency is proven wrong and the chains of oppression are shattered.
- It unifies diversity by creating work in which everyone can participate. Such work is ongoing, proactive, and builds community.
- Constructive program trains people to live a nonviolent life. Just as training for violent revolt means the use of military weapons; training for Satyagraha means constructive program.

In order for constructive programs to have revolutionary power:

- Be concrete and constructive. Although programs can, and often do have symbolic resonance, they cannot be merely symbolic. (Gandhi's spinning wheel was an ideal combination).
- Try to find "stealth" issues whose significance will be underestimated by the opposition – until its too late.
- Most importantly, tackle "keystone" issues that could weaken the whole system if successful; in other words, actions that significantly undermine the oppressive power's "pillars of support."
- Be constructive whenever possible and resistant when necessary.
- Form a strategic overview that balances constructive and obstructive measures; shifting to one or the other as appropriate.

– Reprinted (and slightly adapted) from the Metta Center for Nonviolence's website.

Discussion Questions:
(Time: 5mins)

- What were some examples of constructive programs in *The Dandelion Insurrection*?
- How did the Dandelion Insurrection use constructive programs to empower themselves and weaken their reliance on their opposition?
- Describe some moments when the constructive programs of the Dandelion Insurrection confronted the opposition. (Hint: the story of the Alternet contains some classic examples.)
- What might some other forms of constructive programs have been for the Dandelion Insurrection?

Exercise: Constructive Programs for Your Community or Cause
(Time: 20mins)

Materials: Notebooks and pens.

Facilitators: Ask everyone in the group to take out a notebook and pen. Ask the participants, what is an issue in your community, region, or nation that you are interested in addressing? (Alternatively, what is a cause you are currently engaged in?) Write down your answer. If you have more than one, choose one for the purposes of this exercise.

Next, go around in a quick circle, and ask participants to state their issue or cause. For the next part of the exercise, participants can work individually, in pairs, or in small groups (no more than five). Ask everyone to choose one of those options and find a space in the room to gather in.

Constructive programs are based on cooperating with good while noncooperating with the destructive. Often, our movement or community is dependent on our opposition (or the pillars of support for our opposition) for some, if not all, of their basic needs. In their groups, pairs, or on their own, ask participants to turn to Appendix D: Table For Constructive Programs exercise on page 107.

Appendix D is a table which helps us examine the basic needs of a community and where potential constructive programs may be found. In the left hand column are ten basic needs. (Please add to this list if you think of more.) Fill in the chart with a yes or no answer to the following questions:

- Is this basic need lacking in our community or movement? (Or, is this basic need being fulfilled in a destructive, harmful, or unacceptable manner?)
- Could fulfilling the need strengthen our community or movement?
- Do we depend on the opposition to fulfill this need? If the movement satisfied the need would we lessen our dependency on the opposition?
- Would fulfilling the need weaken our opposition?
- Does fulfilling the need directly resolve the issue or confront the current system that causes the issue?
- Can everyone (or at least a large number of people) participate?

Facilitators: After people have had a chance to fill in their charts, reconvene the whole group and ask people to share some of their discoveries.

- Did you find a perfect potential constructive program?
- Did you find some possibilities that may need careful consideration, but might work if planned correctly? What were they?
- Did you find any surprises?
- Did you discover a basic need that fit the bill except that it does not directly

confront the issue? Would this still be a good project that could strengthen the movement?

Crafting Constructive Programs

Facilitators: Invite the participants to return to their small groups or pairs and ask the following questions:

- What will it take to begin the program?
- What are the barriers to implementation?
- How might the movement build mass participation?
- What legal, political, and other challenges might it face?
- How will the general public view this?
- Will these views change as the program continues?
- When, where, and how might the opposition react to stop the program?
- How will the movement defend and persevere with the program?
- Can the movement use the opposition's attempt to stop the program as "fuel for the fire"? (The Aikido Effect)

Sharing Our Constructive Programs As Stories
(Time: 5-10mins for creating the story; 30mins for sharing the stories)

Facilitators: After the participants have time to discuss and think about the following questions, invite them to spend a few minutes bringing together all of this information into a short (2-5min) story about their constructive program.

- What is the constructive program?
- How does it relate to the movement, the issue, and the community?
- How did it begin, grow, and evolve?
- How did the program strengthen the movement?
- How did the opposition try to stop it?
- How did the movement persevere?
- When all is said and done, what was the outcome?

Example: The Story of Our Local Solar Grids
(This is fiction . . . until you try it!)

We were concerned about climate change and wanted to end the use of fossil fuels. In our community, energy was plentiful, but it came from an unacceptable source: coal. Our electric utility refused to convert, so, given the timeline of climate change, we decided that as a community, we had to take matters into our own hands.

We decided to install local, community solar grids in our neighborhoods and homes. We were not a registered utility, so we had to do an act of civil disobedience to the unjust laws that gave our electric utility a monopoly over our power supply. Together, the communities raised money to establish a revolving loan fund for the solar grids. (The bank would not lend us the money because of the civil disobedience component.) We gathered with our shovels and cement mixers, and a few solar technicians who would lead the project. Everyone participated and it was so much fun! The families on that grid paid into the loan fund which financed the next grid, and so on.

The public utility fought back. A court issued an injunction to stop the installations. We continued despite it. The police came to arrest us as we were working. Another wave of people took over the shovels. We made the front page news, and brought the issue to a head. People said we should have petitioned the utility to convert to solar. We replied that it had been tried and it was time to do something different.

We went through several months of confrontations every weekend. There were lawsuits. We continued installing solar panels. We changed tactics slightly and installed ready-to-be-connected panels everywhere. The police could not arrest us for setting up infrastructure . . . only for trying to connect it to the public power grid or setting up our own power grid. When we had 65% of the town ready to go, we decided to take a stand against the injustice: either the public utility would negotiate with the movement and convert to our local solar grid . . . or we would connect our solar panels as an independent grid and launch a boycott of their power.

The public utility, under pressure from politicians and the public, conceded. We were slightly disappointed at not being able to fire up our independent grid, but we remembered Gandhi's deep understanding of negotiable and non-negotiable issues. We wanted our power to come from solar, not coal. The independency of the grid was a secondary issue. (We have plans to make our public utility a truly public enterprise, but that's another story.)

Facilitators, after giving participants a chance to scribble down some notes about their constructive programs, reconvene the whole group and give everyone a chance to briefly tell their story. Invite reflections at the end of everyone's sharing.

Session Conclusion

Facilitators: Thank the group for their thoughts and comments. We have crossed over the mountain of strategic planning. We have learned to set aims and objectives for the movement, analyze the situation to understand the Pillars of Support, Spectrum of Allies, S.W.O.T. of the opposition and the movement. We have learned how to identify potential campaigns, craft basic campaign designs, assess the risks and advantages, and formulate a preliminary concept of sequence! We have also learned how to craft constructive programs to support and assist our other nonviolent actions. That's pretty darn impressive, don't you think?

Next week, we'll be looking at a variety of other considerations and action-level details. Remind the group of the date, time, and location of the session. Ask them to read the next section in preparation for the discussions next week.

Closing: Facilitators, invite someone to read the quote below. Then go around the circle and ask each participant to share whether they would consider using constructive programs in a struggle they are involved in and why.

"This is our real work," Inez said to Zadie one night. "On the surface, we are planting gardens and growing food, but at the roots we are growing people. We strengthen health through good food, bodies through honest work, minds through education, and hearts and souls through action." – The Dandelion Insurrection

One Billion Rising, Feb 2013, Taos, NM. Photo by Dariel Garner.

Session Six: Tactics, Actions, Message

"Be like the dandelions, courageous bold defenders of the golden soul of humanity, fearless in the face of adversity!" - The Dandelion Insurrection

Greetings, everyone! This week, we'll be getting down into the nitty-gritty of actions . . . which often are the most fun and exciting part of being involved in a movement. And, since action-level strategy is where you decide what signs and banners to paint, we'll also take a look at how to use widely-held values as a foundation for powerful messages that build participation in the movement.

Facilitators: Welcome everyone to today's session. Do a quick check-in about any thoughts or questions that emerged for the group during the past week. Then let's start by asking the group to discuss the difference between tactics and actions.

Reading: The Difference Between Tactics and Actions

Up until now, this study guide has only briefly dealt with the difference between tactics and actions. In much literature around nonviolent struggles, the two terms are used interchangeably or without making a distinction. However, there is one!

An **action** is a specific nonviolent action used at a particular place, time, and location. For example, in *The Dandelion Insurrection*, a group of women lifted their shirts in a public location, revealing dandelion pasties and yelled, "The Dandelion Insurrection is here!"

A **tactic** is a set of actions that share an *approach* and may include several variations on a theme. To take the above example, a *tactic* of dandelion symbols revealed on bare skin could have several variations, each of which becomes an action. The tactic is revealing dandelion symbols on bare skin. Specific actions as part of this tactic might include:

Josie Lenwell's citizen arrest of Donald Rumsfeld (right).

- People of all genders dropping their drawers in a shopping mall on Black Friday at noon and mooning the crowd with dandelions.
- A group of people doing a slow strip tease behind the stage of a political event with dandelions on every layer of skin revealed.
- A student dropping off his graduation robes during Pomp and Circumstance to run naked through the audience with a dandelion painted on his back.

- A veteran opening a raised, clenched fist during the 4th of July Parade to reveal a dandelion symbol on his palm.

Actions are specific to place, time, location, and other details. **Tactics** encompass variations on themes. To be even more specific, this example from *The Dandelion Insurrection* could be described as being part of a **campaign** to do civil disobedience to make the unjust law of banning the symbol of the dandelion unenforceable through mass noncooperation. In this campaign, there were a number of tactics, including spray painting, artist exhibitions, flags, television ads, children's drawings, and more.

Why is this important? In today's session, we're going to work with a resource called a "Tactic Star". It uses both words - tactic and action - so it is helpful to understand the difference between them.

(Disclaimer: it is very common in our real-life movements to hear these terms used without distinction. Stay true to these definitions, and let's help our culture of nonviolent action become more specific in our language.)

"Protect our Salish Sea", Backbone Campaign on the march wtih Idle No More in Seattle, WA, 2014. Photo used with permission from Bill Moyer.

Exercise: Tactic Star - Choosing Actions That Fit the Campaign and Serve the Grand Strategy of the Movement
(Time: 30mins)

Materials: Participants will need a notebook and pen.

A number of considerations go into choosing actions that suit the strategic objectives or goals of a campaign. The War Resisters' International's excellent book, *The Handbook for Nonviolent Campaigns*, shares this helpful "Tactic Star" for examining an action step-by-step to make sure it is appropriate.

Facilitators: Ask the group to pair up or form small groups. For this exercise, we are going to imagine that we are part of the Dandelion Insurrection. In our city or town, we are planning an action as part of a campaign that the nationwide Dandelion Insurrection movement has undertaken. This action is a variation on a theme - part of a tactical approach. Example tactics and campaigns include:

- Victory Gardens as part of the Victory Gardens constructive program campaign
- Altars as part of a campaign around the missing, arrested, or killed friends
- Cazerolazo demonstrations in the campaign to end martial law
- Dandelion Symbols in the campaign to protect the Freedom of Speech
- Not A Terrorist Signs in the campaign to end the witch hunt for Zadie
- TV Smashings in the same campaign above

Ask each pair or group to think up an action they could do in their town or city. For example:

- Plant a Victory Garden in the public park
- Build an altar to missing, beaten, arrested, or killed friends on a fence
- Take our cazerolazo protest out of our homes into the streets
- Make sidewalk chalk paintings of dandelions all throughout town

Each pair or group will work through the Tactic Star below, answering the questions in relation to their proposed action. One person in the pair or group should take notes. The pair or group should revise their proposed action according to the considerations the Tactic Star raises. Perhaps their action is perfect, and perhaps a few adjustments could make it a much stronger, safer action.

The Tactic Star is a tool that leads us through a series of critical questions to help us plan actions that are strategic, effective and purposeful. Follow the star clockwise, from the top ('goals and strategy') using the questions to refine the plan for an action as you go.

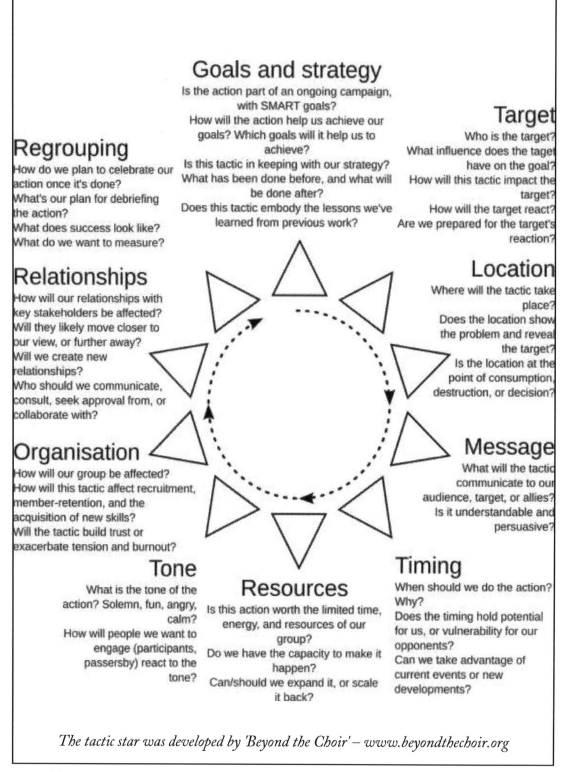

Goals and strategy

Is the action part of an ongoing campaign, with SMART goals?
How will the action help us achieve our goals? Which goals will it help us to achieve?
Is this tactic in keeping with our strategy?
What has been done before, and what will be done after?
Does this tactic embody the lessons we've learned from previous work?

Target

Who is the target?
What influence does the target have on the goal?
How will this tactic impact the target?
How will the target react?
Are we prepared for the target's reaction?

Regrouping

How do we plan to celebrate our action once it's done?
What's our plan for debriefing the action?
What does success look like?
What do we want to measure?

Location

Where will the tactic take place?
Does the location show the problem and reveal the target?
Is the location at the point of consumption, destruction, or decision?

Relationships

How will our relationships with key stakeholders be affected?
Will they likely move closer to our view, or further away?
Will we create new relationships?
Who should we communicate, consult, seek approval from, or collaborate with?

Message

What will the tactic communicate to our audience, target, or allies?
Is it understandable and persuasive?

Organisation

How will our group be affected?
How will this tactic affect recruitment, member-retention, and the acquisition of new skills?
Will the tactic build trust or exacerbate tension and burnout?

Tone

What is the tone of the action? Solemn, fun, angry, calm?
How will people we want to engage (participants, passersby) react to the tone?

Resources

Is this action worth the limited time, energy, and resources of our group?
Do we have the capacity to make it happen?
Can/should we expand it, or scale it back?

Timing

When should we do the action? Why?
Does the timing hold potential for us, or vulnerability for our opponents?
Can we take advantage of current events or new developments?

The tactic star was developed by 'Beyond the Choir' – www.beyondthechoir.org

Note: This tactic star refers to SMART goals. For your reference, that stands for Specific, Measureable, Achievable, Realistic, and Time Bound. You can learn more about this in the War Resisters' International *Handbook for Nonviolent Campaigns*.

Facilitators: Let the pairs or groups know when they have five minutes left. When time is up, reconvene the whole group and open a discussion of how the Tactic Star did or did not alter their concept for their action.

Conclusion: Actions are the bread-and-butter of nonviolent movements for change. For optimal nutrition, they should be part of a well-balanced diet. Strategic planning on all three levels of the movement, campaigns, and actions builds the movement's capacity to wage struggle and win! Next, let's look at a special type of action: the dilemma action.

Reading: Dilemma Actions - Between a Rock and a Hard Place

"Like a good playwright, the tactical artist uses imagination to create choices that are fine for the campaign but bad for the opponent." - George Lakey on dilemma actions, How to Create a Dilemma, Waging Nonviolence.org

"In 2009, the people of Iran went on their rooftops to shout 'Allah Akbar' (God is great) as a protest against the regime. In response, the government had two choices, neither very attractive: let the protest continue unhindered (and possibly grow), or arrest people and try to justify forbidding people shouting that 'God is Great', something commonly done by devout Muslims. This protest is an example of a dilemma action." - Majken Jul Sørensen and Brian Martin, Handbook for Nonviolent Campaigns, War Resisters' International

Dilemma actions put the opponent between a rock and a hard place. No matter what choice the opponent makes, the movement achieves an advantage. Usually the best option for the opponents is to stop the action without anybody noticing. For this reason, many dilemma actions are designed to capture media and public attention, forcing the opponent to make a choice. Generally speaking, a dilemma action is something initiated by the nonviolent movement, rather than a reactive action to something the opponent has done.

Creating a dilemma
(from the Handbook for Nonviolent Campaigns, pg. 129-130.)

Five factors can frequently be found in actual dilemma actions that add to the difficulty of opponents making choices:

-   The action has a constructive, positive element, such as delivering humanitarian aid, or expressing religious commitment, as in Iran in 2009.
-   Activists use surprise or unpredictability, for instance by inventing a new method, or turning up in a totally unexpected place.
-   Opponents' prime choices are in different domains (political, social, personal), which means that the choices are difficult to compare. For example, when a police officer has to choose whether or not to arrest a friend at a

demonstration, there is a conflict between the economic (keep the job), and interpersonal (keep the friend) domains.
- Dilemma actions can be timed to appeal to mass media coverage.
- A dilemma action can appeal to widely held beliefs within society. The apparent religious commitment among the rooftop protesters in Iran is a good example.

Discussion Questions:
(Time: 5-10mins)

- What are some dilemma actions in *The Dandelion Insurrection*?
- Dilemma actions can also be presented by the opposition. What are a few moments in *The Dandelion Insurrection* when the opposition forced Charlie and Zadie in between rocks and hard places?

Conclusion: Dilemma actions are one of the unusual and creative aspects of nonviolent struggle. They are powerful and interesting methods of nonviolent action to have in your toolkit for nonviolent struggle.

Facilitators: Thank everyone for their thoughts and insights. Share with everyone that we are now going to explore the role of values, images, and messaging for a movement.

Values, Image, and Messaging

"Truth is a mighty deep river. Don't get stuck on the surface."
- The Dandelion Insurrection

Reading: Finding Effective Messaging

If the first dynamic of nonviolent struggle is that it grows and succeeds through building mass participation, then how the movement presents itself and its ideas to the public is a pivotal aspect of strategy.

At every phase of a movement, in every campaign and action, the people working on messaging and public presentation should understand the objectives of the grand strategy, as well as the campaign and action level strategies. If the goal of a march is to build mass participation, then the messaging and even the route that is chosen may be different than if the goal is to publically move the participants to a site of occupation.

Sign by LJ Prip.

The ways that the movement presents itself in signs, banners, slogans, interviews, radio shows, and news reports is as important as its other actions and should be approached strategically.

In Chapter 22, Charlie, Zadie, and a team of media people discuss the image and messaging of the Dandelion Insurrection. Due to the control of the conventional media by their opposition, the Dandelion Insurrection has been forced to develop alternative media sources for the movement and the people. The silver lining is that the Dandelion Insurrection has direct control over the information that goes out via the Alternet, the underground media, and Charlie's writings. In this scene, the characters decide to use this strength to focus on the Dandelion Insurrection, rather than on the terrible deeds of their opposition; to build courage and vision instead of fear and hatred; and to humanize the Dandelion Insurrection with images and stories.

Sign at Occupy Eugene, 2011. Photo by David Geitgey Sierralupe.

Discussion Questions:
(Time: 5mins)

- How did the decision to focus on vision, beauty, and widely-held values help the Dandelion Insurrection?
- What slogans, catch phrases, and images did the Dandelion Insurrection use?
- How did these slogans, etc. help to build mass participation and humanize the movement?

Reading: Framing the Struggle

"We're not resisting them! They're resisting us!"
- The Dandelion Insurrection

In that one phrase (above), Zadie reframed the Dandelion Insurrection from a handful of out-powered resisters to the bedrock of humanity. She said, in effect, "We are sane, normal, rational. We are what gives birth to life and continues it onward through time. Our cause is sensible . . . in fact, it is incredibly ordinary to want to live and love. It is our opposition that is behaving egregiously and violating the sanctity of life. The opposition has managed to grasp the power positions of our society, but we outnumber them and we will win - or else they'll die along with everyone else."

Discussion Questions:
(Time: 5mins)

- This is an example of framing (or reframing) the issue. What is the effect of this reframing on the listeners, both the fictional general public in *The Dandelion Insurrection* and yourselves as readers.
- Can you think of examples in your own lives or in struggles you've read about where the movement successfully reframed the issue? How did they do it?

Exercise: Myth - Reality - Widely-held Value
(Time: 30mins)

Materials: A flipchart of paper or a wipe-off board, markers. Later, participants will need a notebook and pen.

Identifying common values shared by the movement and the society helps build participation and support for the movement. During the Civil Rights Movement, participants used words such as *respect, freedom, dignity,* and *equality.* We've all seen opposition groups doing this - the government wrapping a war for profit in the flag of freedom and democracy, or the oil and gas company using phrases like *safe, leadership, freedom of energy independence.* Often, they are using these terms to conceal the truth. A movement for change must use widely-held values not to conceal the truth, but to *reveal* it in powerful ways.

Facilitators: The following exercise can be used to examine the beliefs that divide and unite people around an issue. From this, one can develop effective messages, slogans, and catch phrases for campaigns. Apply this exercise to *The Dandelion Insurrection*, then if your group has time, split into small groups, choose an issue each group is working on (fracking, climate justice, police brutality, poverty and income inequality), apply the exercise to the issue, and see what you can discover. On the flipchart or wipe-off board, layout three columns that look like this:

Myth	Reality	Value

This exercise is adapted from a version presented by Philippe Duhamel. Originally, this tool comes from the late Bill Moyer, a long-time US activist who worked with Martin Luther King's Civil Rights Movement, the Anti-Nuclear movement and many other social movements in the US. The exercise was adapted by Philippe Duhamel for the New Tactics Project's Asia Regional Training Workshop in Thailand (2005), using information from George Lakey (Training for Change).

Next, invite the group to use their own words to explain the three concepts of myth, reality, and widely-held value.

The **Myth** is an idea or assumption (sometimes reinforced by the media or powerful groups) that serves to hide or rationalize an unacceptable situation.

The **Reality** is quite different from the Myth. While the reality is often quite obvious for those living under the weight of it, the Myth hides that reality to the rest of the population or the mainstream. That Reality is often quite outrageous, and that is why we want to change it.

Veterans for Peace Conference, Asheville, NC, 2014. Photo by Josie Lenwell.

That is where the **Widely-held Value** comes in. We need to anchor our message in deep-seated values already held by the mainstream or the sectors of population we want to affect. Careful: we are not talking about the ideas, language or jargon held mainly by activists here, but about a value held and understood by our aunts, our uncles, our neighbours, our average person. When this value is understood clearly, without further explanation by almost everybody, we can use the value like a lever. The widely-held value provides us with powerful leverage.

Next, fill out the columns together, using *The Dandelion Insurrection* as an example. In the novel, the government used many myths to maintain its position. The reality behind those myths was generally stark and frightening. List one myth, the corresponding reality, and the widely-held value that is being violated by the actions of the government in *The Dandelion Insurrection*. Please do not list a whole column full of myths. Instead, stick with one myth, find its corresponding reality, and identify the value that is being violated or threatened before moving onto the next one.

Photo from Anita Stewart.

Some myths and realities may be hard to pin down a one-word value for. Keep at it! Write a few sentences to see if you can discover something essential hiding in the dichotomy between the myth and the reality. The values you uncover are the rallying cries of your movement. What does the Dandelion Insurrection want? Life, liberty, and love! Why do they resist the government? Because the corporate-controlled government wants to destroy those three things that the populace holds dear. Values are what move people into action. Find a value, and you can change the world!

Here are a few examples to get the juices rolling.

Myth	Reality	Value(s)
Business fuels the economy	The owners are stealing everything, and the people are getting poorer.	Fairness Equality Justice
We are a democracy	A hidden dictatorship is controlling everything	Democracy
What's good for the soldiers is good for us all.	Civilian, peaceful societies have different requirements. Martial law and military rule are not good for people.	Freedom
Climate change is nothing to get hot and bothered about.	Climate change could cause the extinction of our entire species!	Life
Terrorism justifies totalitarian measures.	Fear of terrorism is destroying the very civil liberties that Americans want to protect.	Liberty
The government will take care of you.	The corporate-controlled government is willing to cause harm to you and your family to get what it wants.	Love

Facilitators: After the group has filled out the chart with many examples, invite them to consider the following questions.

Discussion Questions:

- What did you learn from this exercise?
- Do those widely-held values resonate with you? What would your aunt, brother, or neighbor think about those values? Do they share them?
- If your employer, co-workers, or the washing machine repairman saw you carrying a sign that said, "Stop Fracking!" what might they think? What might their reaction be if they saw you carrying a sign that read, "We all deserve clean water"?
- Think about an issue you are working on or care about in your own life. What is a myth about that issue? What is the reality? What is the widely-held value?

- What might a slogan or message crafted around a widely-held value on this issue be?

Facilitators: You may wish to take those last two discussion questions a step further. If so, then invite the group to break in to small groups around various issues. (Example, form one group for climate change, another for poverty, and a third for corporate control, etc.) Give the small groups time to explore the Myth - Reality - Widely-held Value Exercise for that issue. Allow them to discuss potential messages, then reconvene the whole group and share

Session Conclusion

While messaging and widely-held values can be identified at any time in the movement, it is on the action level that they will be implemented, perceived, and, hopefully, made effective. Tactical and action level strategy is the most detail oriented of all three levels of strategy.

Facilitators: Thank everyone for their great work today! Remind the group of the date, time, and location of the session. Ask them to read the next section in preparation for the discussion next week. Encourage people to bring snacks and a favorite quote about nonviolence to share.

Closing: Facilitators, please ask someone to read the following quote aloud. Then, ask the group to go around in the circle and say in a few words, what they see coming on the horizon beyond the darkness of today.

"Every morning, the sun rises on a whole new world. Look at what is coming on the horizon. Tell that story!"

– The Dandelion Insurrection

We're as vast as the planet and as microscopic as infectious disease. We aren't a handful of radicals . . . we're all of Life, itself!"
– The Dandelion Insurrection

Peaceful Revolution, Germany, A demonstration on 30 October 1989 in front of Plauen's town hall, Bundesarchiv, Bild 183-1989-1106-405 / CC-BY-SA, via Wikimedia Commons

Session Seven: Bringing People Together

"Let's go rally the dandelions of the soul and stop this madness before it begins!"
– The Dandelion Insurrection

Welcome everyone! This week, we're moving beyond the nuts and bolts of strategy into the staples of organizing. It's one thing to have a brilliant strategic plan. It's another to have the people power to implement it. In this section, we'll be exploring some very basic concepts of how to bring people together.

Facilitators: This section is structured in a series of discussions. Simply ask the discussion questions (and any others that occur to you) and allow the conversation to unfold.

Reading: Cookies and Community

"If you want to do something truly radical, be kind, be connected, be unafraid!"
– The Dandelion Insurrection

We have all been organizers at one point or another. Perhaps we rallied the school kids for a game of tag. Or maybe we spearheaded the fundraiser for the local charity. Some of us have organized family reunions and weddings, or hosted Superbowl Sunday parties. Organizing is a very common human activity that involves coordinating the details (who, what, where, when, why, how) and gathering the people.

Organizing for action can be done in many ways, but I'll give you a hint: those who organize with a sense of community and fun tend to build participation quickly. Potlucks, kindness, and patience are useful ingredients to building a successful movement. Yes, it is important for the mothers to discuss their children for ten minutes before the meeting starts . . . those children are often the motivating factor that brings the mothers to the meetings.

"We've got to wash the tired minds of the public in reminders of why life is worth living. No ounce of beauty is too small to share."
– The Dandelion Insurrection

Black Lives Matter, All Lives Matter demonstration in DC, 2014. Photo by Josie Lenwell.

Personal Story: Love-In-Action Network

The same month that *The Dandelion Insurrection* was published, my partner, a friend, and I formed the Love-In-Action Network to help foster local nonviolent action study and strategy groups. Here in Taos, New Mexico, where I live, our local Love-In-Action group has been organizing nonviolent actions and awareness-building events for a variety of issues since March 2014. We began with homemade cookies and conversation. At first, there were three of us. Now, in our small mountain town of 4,000 people, we gather 12-30 people regularly, expanding that number when we plan actions or demonstrations.

We gather every other Monday, discuss local and national issues, study nonviolent action (using some of the exercises in this study guide, among others), and plan local actions. We provide support, feedback, and creativity to each other's endeavors. We use creativity and our heartfelt passion for life to create beautiful actions and plan wise strategies. My long-term dream is that every community has a Love-In-Action group that meets regularly and shares the tools of nonviolent action. If you would like to form a group to continue to deepen your understanding and application of nonviolent action, visit the website: www.loveinactionnet.com

Discussion Questions:
(Time: 20 mins)

- What have you organized in your life? (potlucks, fundraisers, family vacations, social justice movements, community efforts to improve playgrounds)
- What have you learned from those experiences about bringing people together, planning an endeavor, and taking action as a group?
- In *The Dandelion Insurrection*, what were some ways that people organized? Explore how the different groups in the book gathered people together - the Suburban Renaissance, Inez' urban communities, Rudy's town, Charlie's relatives up north, Ellen and Bill's Dandelion Farm, etc.
- If you are organizing for action in your community, take a moment to reflect and share on what works for you and what seems to be a challenge. If you are not currently organizing, share some reflections about what you think might be a good way to start bringing people together.

Reading: Leadership and Self-Organizing Structures

"When everyone knows how to plan, you start to see strategic behavior."
- Ivan Marovic, Otpor!

Leadership and organizing structure for nonviolent movements has been a subject of intense debate for decades. There are many different schools and theories. In *The Dandelion Insurrection*, the characters work with a "leader-full" structure. The Occupy protests called this the "leaderless" model, but as I say in the novel:

"This system has been called leaderless," Zadie said, "but I see it more as leader-full. If every person thoroughly understands the overarching strategy and is empowered to lead, then you've got innovation and organization working together effectively, creating a tremendous explosion of activity without a chain of command." - The Dandelion Insurrection

This system has many historical examples, including the student group, Otpor! that ousted Milosevic from power. Long after writing *The Dandelion Insurrection*, I had an opportunity to attend a seminar with Ivan Marovic, who was part of Otpor! and described how general systems theory and self-regulating systems influenced how they organized.

"General systems theory is the interdisciplinary study of systems in general, with the goal of elucidating principles that can be applied to all types of systems at all nesting levels in all fields of research." - Wikipedia

That sounds like a mouthful, and it is. Systems theorists look at the principles and dynamics that describe how a system (like an ecosystem or economy) works. They also examine how fish school, bees swarm, birds flock . . . and how change happens. In my personal opinion, some of the oldest scholars of systems theory are the Taoists. The I-Ching contains sixty-four descriptions of how change happens. The Buddhists also have a long history of examining the interconnected web of systems and the causal links in that web.

My personal introduction to systems theory came through modern dance improvisation. In a dance ensemble class, we were asked to experiment with the principles that drove the "murmurations" of flocking starlings.

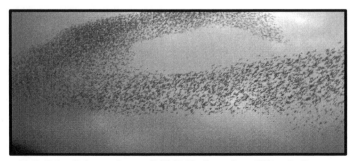

"The starlings only have a few rules: fly forward, the leader changes at every shift in direction, keep equidistant, and don't leave your wing-mate out on a limb."
- The Dandelion Insurrection

By D. Dibenski (images.fws.gov ([1])) [Public domain], via Wikimedia Commons

As human dancers, we followed these rules. Lo and behold, a murmuration emerged. The starlings use the murmurations to escape and drive away predatory hawks. In terms of numbers and power dynamics, the murmuration offers a great parallel for people's movements. We have a few powerful hawks hunting down people. One by one, our fellow starlings are getting picked off or chased to exhaustion. If we unite, organize a movement, and learn to work strategically, we can give those hawks a run for their money and protect our families and friends.

The murmuration is an example of what systems theorists call a "self-regulating structure". Activists call it a "leaderless" movement. *The Dandelion Insurrection* calls it a leader-full movement. There are a few key elements of creating a successful self-organizing movement:

- Clear aims and objectives (otherwise, your flock is flying in 10 directions at once)
- Established principles that guide the movement (ex: a commitment to nonviolence)
- Widespread strategic knowledge of nonviolent struggle.
- An accessible training process that introduces participants to all of the above.

There is also a theory of a "cloud" formation, which is a subject of intense debate around my house whenever the phrase "the Movement of Movements" comes up. The theory is that a swarm of groups working roughly toward similar goals could successfully undermine the stranglehold of power held by a small, but powerful set of people - even if those groups are not overtly working on a shared strategy. My partner calls this the "cloud" formation. Having grown up in Maine, I envision a hoard of mosquitos driving a 2,000 pound moose insane.

The cloud formation varies from the murmuration model in that the individuals and groups may not share principles, aims, objectives, or training process. However, Ivan Marovic's quote still applies:

"When everyone knows how to plan, you start to see strategic behavior." - Ivan Marovic, Otpor!

Discussion Questions:
(Time: 25mins)

- What are your thoughts on the role of leadership in a nonviolent movement?
- Have you been a part of a so-called leaderless movement? What were some advantages and disadvantages?

- Have you seen the models of murmurations or cloud formations in action anywhere in your life? Where? What was it like?
- Are there other system models (schools of fish, erupting volcanoes, ecosystems) that you might use to organize a nonviolent action, campaign, or movement? What would that look like?
- What were the guiding principles of *The Dandelion Insurrection*? Would you have added or removed any of these principles?
- In *The Dandelion Insurrection*, the characters discussed self-organizing structures. What are the four mechanisms of self-organizing structures that help them grow and replicate?
- What forms of leadership and organization have you found most satisfying in your own personal experiences? Conversely, what forms haven't worked well for you, and why?

Conclusion: By using shared aims, objectives, and principles and by building widespread strategic knowledge, a movement can be self-organizing and leader-full. Otpor!'s organizational model also offers insight into movement growth, which we will look at next.

Reading: A.R.T. - Learning from Serbia's Otpor!

Otpor! was a Serbian pro-democracy movement. When it formed in 1998, it was only a handful of students. By 2000, Otpor! had more than 70,000 active participants and managed to overthrow Milosevic during the October 2000 elections.

How did they grow so fast?

According to Ivan Marovic, a member of Otpor!, the group was a self-organizing structure built on principles of general systems theory. They created replicable guidelines for each chapter of Otpor!,

Otpor! recruitment flier.

established clear objectives and grand strategy, and allowed each chapter to exercise creativity and a certain amount of autonomy. There were no designated leaders in Otpor! - a problem if groups began to act in a way that other Otpor! members did not agree with. Instead of the core leaders authoritatively stating the laws, the participants had to go speak with one another and debate the wisdom of the approach until changes of viewpoints occurred.

The secret to their rapid growth lies in the A.R.T. cycle - which is my acronym for Otpor!'s

Action, Recruitment, Training process.

Action: Every weekend, Otpor! groups would organize a street action - a demonstration or rally or other creative action, often with lots of humor involved. At the action, people would naturally ask the students who they were and what they were doing. These questions became opportunities to recruit new people to the movement.

Recruitment: At these actions, Otpor! member designated "recruiters" whose task was to have these dialogues and if a person was interested, collect contact information. The person would be invited to the training happening on Monday, and the Otpor! recruiter would telephone the person the next day to remind him or her about the training.

Training: Otpor! hosted trainings Monday thru Friday 7-8:30pm, every week. Imagine! The 5-day course was cumulative and mandatory for all potential Otpor! members. Why? Because this was where the essential information about Otpor! was taught. These trainings were what ensured that Otpor! would be Otpor! no matter who was organizing in any region of Serbia. This is not the only model for organizing, but it is a useful one to analyze and see what can be adapted in your community. Let's look at what Otpor! taught each night.

Day 1: Basics of Otpor! On the first day, Otpor! trainers introduced newcomers to the basics: who we are, what we do, definitions of nonviolence, and what the grand strategy is (bring down Milosevic via the 2000 elections). At the end of the night, participants would be given the choice to complete the next four days of training, or say "this movement is not for me". If the person wanted to move forward, they would have to agree to accept the rules of the movement and the grand strategy.

Day 2: Basic Recruitment Skills. Otpor! trained people immediately to recruit other people, how to explain the movement, the purpose, and the nonviolent strategy; how to collect contact information and excite people about Otpor!'s work. This is an essential ingredient to the A.R.T. cycle as you will soon see.

Day 3: How to Talk to the Media. Otpor! trained every single member on media relations. They would also role play interviews for radio, print, and television. With no official leaders, it was important that each person knew how to present Otpor! to the press and public.

Day 4: Basic Elements of Otpor! Branding. Otpor! would teach its members how to paint and print the Otpor! logo, make banners, signs, and messaging. This ensured a uniformity of image between all the various chapters of Otpor!.

Day 5: Learn to Plan a Street Action. On the last day of training, Otpor! members learned the nuts and bolts of how to translate the grand strategy into street actions. These would be primarily symbolic, low-risk nonviolent actions. The planning session would occur on Friday night and the focus would be to plan the action that would occur on Saturday. At the end of the evening, the rules of nonviolence would be revisited and every person participating in the Saturday action would be required to sign a nonviolence commitment.

Saturday Action: On Saturday, the Action - Recruitment - Training cycle would come full circle. New members would take action and recruit the next batch of new members. After the Saturday action - and only afterwards - the newly trained Otpor! members would be fully accepted into the movement and given an Otpor! button to indicate they had completed training.

The A.R.T. cycle worked powerfully for Otpor!, growing the organization from 50 students to over 70,000 students in just two years. (For reference, the total population of Serbia at that time was around 7 million.) The students used creativity, humor, self-organizing structures like those in *The Dandelion Insurrection*, and wise strategy to achieve the success of their movement.

(Ivan Marovic also confessed that each night of training ended with a trip to the bar . . . the Serbian version of cookies and community.)

Discussion Questions:
(Time: 20mins)

- What elements of the A.R.T. cycle helped build the exponential growth of Otpor!?
- How can you imagine applying some of this cycle to your own movement or community?
- What might be the effect in your own community or movement if you started to use the A.R.T. cycle?
- If you could run a weekly training program, what might you include in the curriculum?
- What might be the effect in your movement if everyone knew the aims, objectives, grand strategy, campaign sequences, and guiding principles of the movement?
- How might you tweak the Otpor! model to work in your own situation?

Kids & parents carry a 40ft purple dragon made of recycled materials for Earth Day 2014. Taos, NM

Conclusion: Facilitators, thank everyone for their comments and participation. Next, we're going to discuss the importance of roles in a movement.

Reading: A Place for Everyone - The Importance of Roles

In a nonviolent movement, there are literally hundreds of ways people can participate. From answering emails and telephone calls to updating social media accounts, to fielding press interviews, to designing fliers, to strategizing actions, to providing legal assistance; a nonviolent movement requires many skill sets and levels of involvement. For every person who risks arrest or engages in civil disobedience, the movement may require ten people to do other tasks.

Identifying the diverse ways people can help the movement builds participation. It can provide "safe" roles for people who cannot risk arrest, termination of employment, or expulsion from school, and/or have physical limitations that prevent them from other activities. Giving each person a role to play in the movement also ensures that the movement accomplishes the thousands of mundane, tedious, unnoticed tasks that lay the foundation for successful actions.

LJ Prip, David Soumis, and friend at a peace rally, 2014. Photo courtesy of David Soumis.

Discussion Questions:
(Time: 15mins)

- In *The Dandelion Insurrection*, what were some ways that people became involved in the movement? What were some support roles or small tasks that people did to help the Dandelion Insurrection? How did elders, youths, parents and students get involved?
- What are some roles you would be willing to play in a nonviolent movement for change?
- What are some ways in which your aunt, grandmother, neighbors, the kid down the street, etc. may be able to take part in a nonviolent movement for change?
- In a movement or campaign you are a part of, what are some roles that could be shared? What are some that could be developed or filled?
- If 100 people showed up tomorrow to get involved with the movement, what would you ask them to do? What about 1,000?

Reading: Beyond the Choir - Reaching Out To Others

"There are three hundred million people in this country. Someone has to pull their love from the womb of their hearts and spur them into action."
— The Dandelion Insurrection

Remember the first dynamic of nonviolent struggle? Mass participation is key to the success of nonviolent movements. This means diversity. It means differences. It means respect, deep listening, and being willing to consider the ideas of others.

It also means outreach. The Spectrum of Allies exercise in Session Four is a useful tool for identifying groups to reach out to and work with. You can also find groups that may exist just outside your comfort zone or your ordinary circuit of community interactions.

Discussion Questions:
(Time: 10mins)

- What were some groups that the Dandelion Insurrection involved in their efforts?
- Which of these groups were logical allies, and which were surprises? Which groups were a "stretch" for the Dandelion Insurrection?
- What are some groups or people that could be brought into a movement you are a part of? How and why would they decide to join the movement? What roles would they play?

Chas Schaeffer and young friends at May Day DC 2013, Malcolm X Park. Photo courtesy of Chas Schaeffer.

Campaign Nonviolence Houston, Campaign Nonviolence Week of Actions 2014.
Used with permission from Jerry Monroe Maynard.

Session Conclusion

When we bring people together, we honor our community by listening and respecting the unique strengths of each person. Creating change is hard work . . . but it is worth every effort!

Facilitators: This concludes our session for today. Ask the group to please read the next section. Remind them that this will be our last session with the study guide. Make sure everyone knows the date, time, and location of the next meeting. Next week, we will be looking at reflections on responsibility and moving forward into action!

Closing: Facilitators, ask if anyone remembered to bring their favorite nonviolence quote. If anyone forgot, they could use a favorite quote from *The Dandelion Insurrection.* For today's closing, simply allow each person to share their quote. Then, thank everyone for their presence, spirit, and sharings.

Session Eight: Reflections & Moving Forward!

"As long as life pulsed on the planet, as long as two hearts entwined, as long as a tendril of compassion continued, their legacy in this world was assured."
- The Dandelion Insurrection

Welcome. Today is our last session with *The Dandelion Insurrection Study Guide.* We're going to do a lot of reflecting today, sharing our thoughts on this journey and the path moving forward into action.

Facilitators: This session is set up with discussion questions. You may wish to invite your group to add questions to the conversation today. In your opening, do a quick go-around and see how people are feeling about coming to the end of the study guide sessions. Perhaps people are excited to move into action. Perhaps some might have concerns about taking action. Others may be both excited and nervous at the concept of applying the things we've been discussing. After everyone has spoken a brief sentence or two, open up the discussion questions from this section.

Reading: Reflections on Responsibility

Nonviolent struggles can be invigorating, inspiring, life changing, transformative and empowering. They can also be overwhelming, frightening, dangerous, and exhausting. The Civil Rights Movement, for example, had many "hours of darkness". Records kept by SNCC (Student Nonviolent Coordinating Committee) showed that in a three-month period, from June 16 to September 30, 1964, there were 6 murders, 29 shootings, 50 bombings, and 60 beatings of locals and civil rights workers. Waging struggle is not without dangers. Entering into struggle with a realistic understanding - neither exaggerated nor naive - prepares us to make wise choices along the journey. Considering the potential problems with equal measure to the vision of change is essential for maintaining one's courage and determination for the duration of the struggle.

History has shown that, compared to violent conflicts, using nonviolent methods decreases, but does not eliminate casualties, injuries, loss of property, wealth, livelihood, and liberty for the individuals involved. *The Dandelion Insurrection* is a fictional depiction of such struggles, but, as an author, I tried to portray the struggle somewhat realistically. In the novel, Charlie and Zadie grapple with their responsibility for starting a nonviolent struggle against a tyrannical, violent regime. They question: a) what might happen if they move people into action, and b) what might happen if they don't!

Discussion Questions:
(Time: 15mins)

- *The Dandelion Insurrection*, even though it is fictional, tries to portray some of the sobering realities along side the more exhilarating moments. What are some challenges the characters faced in *The Dandelion Insurrection*?
- In Chapter Sixteen, Zadie confesses to Charlie that she "invented" the Dandelion Insurrection, misleading him into thinking he was reporting on the movement, when in actuality, he was fomenting it. If you were Charlie, what would your reaction be? Conversely, if you were in Zadie's shoes, would you have chosen her actions or a different set of actions?
- Throughout the novel, Charlie and Zadie face the real costs of their choices to wage nonviolent struggle (imprisonment of loved ones, injuries, death, assaults, fears, loss of freedoms, etc.), not only for themselves, but for everyone they have led into action. How do they grapple with this responsibility? If you were in their position, how would you reflect on these issues?
- In your own lives, how do you feel about the risks you might face in the context of a nonviolent struggle?
- Are there some risks you are willing to take and others you are not? What are they?
- In your movement, you may be a strategist or an organizer, making decisions and plans that could affect many other people. What are your reflections on the responsibility of a strategist or organizer?
- While action comes with consequences, so does passivity. In our current times, how do you feel about your responsibility to take action?

Discussion: Courage, Inspiration, Endurance!

Every struggle for change will encounter "make-or-break" moments or "hours of darkness". Preparing emotional, psychological, and spiritual resources both individually and as a movement may help us navigate these challenging moments. In the next set of discussion questions, let's talk about those hours of darkness, the challenges of being part of a movement, how the characters handled them, and what you would do if faced with a similar challenge.

Discussion Questions: Courage, Inspiration, Endurance!
(Time: 20mins)

- Can you identify some "hour of darkness" or challenging moments for the characters in *The Dandelion Insurrection*?
- What sustained the characters through those times?
- Have you experienced an extreme challenge either in a nonviolent

movement for change or in another aspect of your life? How did you deal with it?

- In your own struggles, where do you find the strength to continue?
- For many people, including the characters in *The Dandelion Insurrection*, faith and spirituality provide a well of strength and solace for their efforts to make change. What are some moments when the characters drew on their faith and spiritual practices for inner strength and outer actions?
- How does your faith influence you (or not)?
- What other types of emotional, psychological, and spiritual resources would you call on when experiencing a difficult time in a nonviolent struggle?

Discussion: Invoking the Lineage

Several times throughout *The Dandelion Insurrection*, the lineage of nonviolence was evoked. Remembering the heroes and sheroes who have worked for justice throughout history is one way to give us courage and strength for the journey.

Discussion Questions: Heroes in the Lineage of Nonviolence
(Time: 20 mins)

- Who are your personal heroes or sheroes who have worked for justice or been involved in nonviolent struggles? Why are they inspirational for you?
- Are there particular historic movements that give you courage for waging struggle today? What were they and how do they inform your choices?
- Who are the currently living and active people who inspire you?

Photo from Anita Stewart, Tampa, FL

Discussion: Moving Forward!

These discussion questions and exercises serve as the bridge between the novel of *The Dandelion Insurrection* and the reality of your own world. This time you have spent with your study group is precious. Take a moment to thank each other for your listening, honesty, and presence during this journey.

Session Conclusion

Facilitators, invite the group to thank one another for the journey of working together through this study guide. Encourage everyone to share gratitude or thoughts that have not yet been expressed. Ask each person to share one thing from this study guide session that he or she will take away into the next steps of their journey. Finally, let's close by standing, joining hands if it feels appropriate, and having someone volunteer to read the closing lines of *The Dandelion Insurrection*.

"Charlie looked at all the people, the millions of faces in this ocean . . . the tide of history ebbed and flowed through their bodies. He watched them sing, saw them cry, caught one smile to another, and his heart broke into infinite shards of compassion. Breath swelled in their chests. Love rippled, surged, and crested. A thought crashed through Charlie like a wave . . .

"We are one people, indivisible, not by allegiance or by force, but entwined through the love in our hearts. Through our pulse, and our breath, and our frail human skins, the body of the people stands immortal. We rise and we fall; we sweep by in waves of faces; we roll in the rushing tide of life. We are foolish, we are proud, we are loving, we are tired; we weep for beauty, laugh in sorrow, cry out lonely in the night; we hurt and cause harm; we are lovers and beloveds; we shall live, we shall die, we shall pass and still remain; for the body of the people lives forever."

– The Dandelion Insurrection

Thank you!

Afterword from Rivera Sun

Drawing by Grace Silvermoon

My friends,

Thank you for taking this journey. We live in times of great change, and I appreciate having many companions on this road. As a human being, it warms my heart to imagine you as one of the thousand points of light shining in the darkness before dawn. It is as if we have gathered to sing the rising sun up from the dark rim of the horizon. With great faith, courage, and connection, we are bringing a new world out of the unworkable shell of the old.

Gandhi called his endeavors "experiments in Truth", a phrase I also enjoy using in my work as an organizer and activist. It evokes open-minded experimentation with making change through nonviolent action, and a sense of humility about my own efforts. Gandhi's Truth is a lofty aspiration, one that we all may reach for, and, in that act of reaching, we may achieve our potential as human beings. With all of our hearts, we reach for that which we believe in, stretching ourselves and society in the direction of equality, justice, respect, freedom, compassion and wisdom.

Today, we stand on the shoulders of giants. The field of nonviolent struggle has been studied and written about by thousands of scholars and practitioners. As you close the final pages of this study guide, I hope you will open the pages of a thousand more volumes, learning as much as you can while putting these ideas into practice.

Your friend and companion on the road of nonviolent change,

Rivera Sun

Quote-pic created by Brian Heater

Appendix A: 198 METHODS OF NONVIOLENT ACTION

Far too often, people struggling for democratic rights and justice are not aware of the full range of methods of nonviolent action. Wise strategy, attention to the dynamics of nonviolent struggle, and careful selection of methods can increase a group's chances of success.

THE METHODS OF NONVIOLENT PROTEST AND PERSUASION

Formal Statements
1. Public Speeches
2. Letters of opposition or support
3. Declarations by organizations and institutions
4. Signed public statements
5. Declarations of indictment and intention
6. Group or mass petitions

Communications with a Wider Audience
7. Slogans, caricatures, and symbols
8. Banners, posters, displayed communications
9. Leaflets, pamphlets, and books
10. Newspapers and journals
11. Records, radio, and television
12. Skywriting and earthwriting

Group Representations
13. Deputations
14. Mock awards
15. Group lobbying
16. Picketing
17. Mock elections

Symbolic Public Acts
18. Displays of flags and symbolic colors
19. Wearing of symbols
20. Prayer and worship
21. Delivering symbolic objects
22. Protest disrobings
23. Destruction of own property
24. Symbolic lights
25. Displays of portraits
26. Paint as protest
27. New signs and names
28. Symbolic sounds
29. Symbolic reclamations
30. Rude gestures

Pressures on Individuals
31. "Haunting" officials

32. Taunting officials
33. Fraternization
34. Vigils
   Drama and Music
35. Humorous skits and pranks
36. Performances of plays and music
37. Singing
   Processions
38. Marches
39. Parades
40. Religious processions
41. Pilgrimages
42. Motorcades
   Honoring the Dead
43. Political mourning
44. Mock funerals
45. Demonstrative funerals
46. Homage at burial places
   Public Assemblies
47. Assemblies of protest or support
48. Protest meetings
49. Camouflaged meetings of protest
50. Teach-ins
   Withdrawal and Renunciation
51. Walk-outs
52. Silence
53. Renouncing honors
54. Turning one's back

THE METHODS OF SOCIAL NONCOOPERATION

Ostracism of Persons
55. Social boycott
56. Selective social boycott
57. Lysistratic nonaction
58. Excommunication
59. Interdict
   Noncooperation with Social Events, Customs, and Institutions
60. Suspension of social and sports activities
61. Boycott of social affairs
62. Student strike
63. Social disobedience
64. Withdrawal from social institutions
   Withdrawal from the Social System
65. Stay-at-home

66. Total personal noncooperation
67. "Flight" of workers
68. Sanctuary
69. Collective disappearance
70. Protest emigration (hijrat)

THE METHODS OF ECONOMIC NONCOOPERATION: ECONOMIC BOYCOTTS

Actions by Consumers
71. Consumers' boycott
72. Nonconsumption of boycotted goods
73. Policy of austerity
74. Rent withholding
75. Refusal to rent
76. National consumers' boycott
77. International consumers' boycott
    Action by Workers and Producers
78. Workmen's boycott
79. Producers' boycott
    Action by Middlemen
80. Suppliers' and handlers' boycott
    Action by Owners and Management
81. Traders' boycott
82. Refusal to let or sell property
83. Lockout
84. Refusal of industrial assistance
85. Merchants' "general strike"
    Action by Holders of Financial Resources
86. Withdrawal of bank deposits
87. Refusal to pay fees, dues, and assessments
88. Refusal to pay debts or interest
89. Severance of funds and credit
90. Revenue refusal
91. Refusal of a government's money
    Action by Governments
92. Domestic embargo
93. Blacklisting of traders
94. International sellers' embargo
95. International buyers' embargo
96. International trade embargo

(continued on next page)

THE METHODS OF ECONOMIC NONCOOPERATION: THE STRIKE

Symbolic Strikes
97. Protest strike
98. Quickie walkout (lightning strike)
   Agricultural Strikes
99. Peasant strike
100. Farm Workers' strike
   Strikes by Special Groups
101. Refusal of impressed labor
102. Prisoners' strike
103. Craft strike
104. Professional strike
   Ordinary Industrial Strikes
105. Establishment strike
106. Industry strike
107. Sympathetic strike
   Restricted Strikes
108. Detailed strike
109. Bumper strike
110. Slowdown strike
111. Working-to-rule strike
112. Reporting "sick" (sick-in)
113. Strike by resignation
114. Limited strike
115. Selective strike
   Multi-Industry Strikes
116. Generalized strike
117. General strike
   Combination of Strikes and Economic Closures
118. Hartal
119. Economic shutdown

THE METHODS OF POLITICAL NONCOOPERATION

Rejection of Authority
120. Withholding or withdrawal of allegiance
121. Refusal of public support
122. Literature and speeches advocating resistance

Citizens' Noncooperation with Government
123. Boycott of legislative bodies
124. Boycott of elections
125. Boycott of government employment and positions
126. Boycott of government depts., agencies, and other bodies

127. Withdrawal from government educational institutions
128. Boycott of government-supported organizations
129. Refusal of assistance to enforcement agents
130. Removal of own signs and placemarks
131. Refusal to accept appointed officials
132. Refusal to dissolve existing institutions

Citizens' Alternatives to Obedience

133. Reluctant and slow compliance
134. Nonobedience in absence of direct supervision
135. Popular nonobedience
136. Disguised disobedience
137. Refusal of an assemblage or meeting to disperse
138. Sitdown
139. Noncooperation with conscription and deportation
140. Hiding, escape, and false identities
141. Civil disobedience of "illegitimate" laws

Action by Government Personnel

142. Selective refusal of assistance by government aides
143. Blocking of lines of command and information
144. Stalling and obstruction
145. General administrative noncooperation
146. Judicial noncooperation
147. Deliberate inefficiency and selective noncooperation by enforcement agents
148. Mutiny

Domestic Governmental Action

149. Quasi-legal evasions and delays
150. Noncooperation by constituent governmental units

International Governmental Action

151. Changes in diplomatic and other representations
152. Delay and cancellation of diplomatic events
153. Withholding of diplomatic recognition
154. Severance of diplomatic relations
155. Withdrawal from international organizations
156. Refusal of membership in international bodies
157. Expulsion from international organizations

THE METHODS OF NONVIOLENT INTERVENTION

Psychological Intervention

158. Self-exposure to the elements
159. The fast
    a)   Fast of moral pressure
    b)   Hunger strike
    c)   Satyagrahic fast

160. Reverse trial
161. Nonviolent harassment
       Physical Intervention
162. Sit-in
163. Stand-in
164. Ride-in
165. Wade-in
166. Mill-in
167. Pray-in
168. Nonviolent raids
169. Nonviolent air raids
170. Nonviolent invasion
171. Nonviolent interjection
172. Nonviolent obstruction
173. Nonviolent occupation
       Social Intervention
174. Establishing new social patterns
175. Overloading of facilities
176. Stall-in
177. Speak-in
178. Guerrilla theater
179. Alternative social institutions
180. Alternative communication system
       Economic Intervention
181. Reverse strike
182. Stay-in strike
183. Nonviolent land seizure
184. Defiance of blockades
185. Politically motivated counterfeiting
186. Preclusive purchasing
187. Seizure of assets
188. Dumping
189. Selective patronage
190. Alternative markets
191. Alternative transportation systems
192. Alternative economic institutions
       Political Intervention
193. Overloading of administrative systems
194. Disclosing identities of secret agents
195. Seeking imprisonment
196. Civil disobedience of "neutral" laws
197. Work-on without collaboration
198. Dual sovereignty and parallel government

Gene Sharp researched and catalogued these 198 methods and provided a rich selection of historical examples in his seminal work, *The Politics of Nonviolent Action* (3 Vols.) Boston: Porter Sargent, 1973.

For further inquiry, please contact
The Albert Einstein Institution
PO Box 455
East Boston, MA 02128
USA
tel: 617.247.4882
fax: 617.247.4035
email: einstein@igc.org
web: www.aeinstein.org

Appendix B: Outline of a Strategic Planning Process

Note: This outline is a suggested process for a strategic planning session for an issue you may be working on (i.e. climate change, income inequality, police brutality, etc.) It is designed for two weekend sessions with 1-2 weeks in between for research. This may seem like a lot of time, but it is time well-spent. This process could be done with a very small to mid-sized group. Choose a quiet, comfortable location, if possible.

Session 1: Weekend One
- Centering and Arriving: welcoming, centering, and establishing ground rules for the session (listening, respect, consensus process, agenda, protocols, note taker, facilitator, etc).
- Broad Aims for the movement: Take time to discuss the Broad Aims of the movement
- Potential Specific Objectives for the movement (be flexible, they may change)
- Analyzing the Situation: use the exercises in this study guide; Pillars of Support, Spectrum of Allies, S.W.O.T. to examine in great detail the movement, your opposition, the problem, the potentials for change, etc. Take as much time as necessary to do this as thoroughly as possible. This process may take you one day or two days. Devote the time. You can adjust the rest of your strategic planning process accordingly.
- Remember to mark your charts with the following labels: W - weakness; S - strength; C - potential campaign.
- Identify Potential Campaigns: list out all the potential campaigns that have been identified in the strategic analysis. Also, make note of any needs that the movement has that have not been framed as campaigns.
- Identify questions that still need to be answered. Delegate the research.
- Take a moment to see if the group can identify a Grand Strategy at this point. If not, come back to this question in the next session.
- Set the time, date, and location for the next session.
- Conclusions, Reflections, Gratitude

Session 2: Weekend 2
- Centering and Arriving: welcoming, centering, and reminding everyone of the ground rules for the session (listening, respect, consensus process, agenda, protocols, note taker, facilitator, etc).
- Review the Analysis: Have the note taker from the first session review the notes of the strategic analysis.
- Ask about the questions that were being researched between the sessions.
- Add new information to Pillars and Spectrum diagrams.
- Pull out the list of potential campaigns.

- Add new potential campaigns to those identified previously.
- Take a moment to reflect on your proposed or still unknown Grand Strategy. Is it possible to articulate one at this point? Do you need to adjust a proposed Grand Strategy that you had already stated? See if you can identify the Grand Strategy before moving forward. If not, continue, but remember that Grand Strategy should inform your campaign design, ordering, and strategies.
- Can you identify your movement's broad aims and specific objectives at this point? Try to articulate them before examining the campaigns.
- Campaign Design: Use the Crafting Cumulative Campaigns Exercise in Session Five of the study guide to examine every potential campaign. Take as much time as you need to explore this. Make notes on the resources, messaging, possible tactics/actions, campaign objectives, potential costs and risks, how it shifts the situation, timing and duration.
- Identify Possible Chronological Order of Campaigns: Use the Ordering Cumulative Campaigns Exercise in Session Five of this Study Guide.
- If necessary, adjust campaign order to include movement-building campaigns to support other types of campaigns. Use the Constructive Programs for Your Community or Cause Exercise in Session Five of this study guide to determine potential constructive programs.
- Messaging: Use Myths - Realities - Values Exercise in Session Six of this study guide to determine some potential messaging, slogans, or images that may be effective for the movement.
- What is missing from analysis? Take some time to examine what has not been explored. See how that might affect previous understandings.
- Implementation: Explore what needs to be done to achieve this plan? Who will do it? Set next steps for implementing the strategic plan.
- Conclusions: Be sure to take time to share reflections, and gratitude for this process.

Appendix C: Resources for Further Study

Organizations:

The Albert Einstein Institution
Website: www.aeinstein.org
Email: einstein@igc.org
Address: P.O. Box 455, Boston, MA 02118
Phone: (617) 247-4882 fax: (617) 247-4035

Backbone Campaign
Website: www.backbonecampaign.org
Email: info@BackboneCampaign.org
Address: Backbone Campaign PO BOX 278, Vashon, WA 98070
Phone: 206-408-8058

International Center on Nonviolent Conflict
Website: www.nonviolent-conflict.org
Email: icnc@nonviolent-conflict.org
Address: P.O. Box 27606
Washington, DC 20038
Phone: USA + 202-416-4720
fax: USA + 202-466-5918

The Metta Center for Nonviolence
Website: www.mettacenter.org
Email: info@mettacenter.org
Phone: 707-774-6299

Pace e Bene and Campaign Nonviolence
Website: www.paceebene.org
Email: info@paceebene.org
Address: Pace e Bene
PO Box 1891
Long Beach, CA 90801
Phone: 510-268-8765
Fax: 702-648-2281

Popular Resistance
Website: www.popularresistance.org
Email: info@popularresistance.org
Phone: 202-688-2444

> These organizations, websites, and books were extremely helpful in developing this study guide. Please use them as you continue your study of nonviolent action both in research and in practice. Thank you!
>
> "Nonviolence is a direction, not a separating line."
>
> - Vietnamese monk and peace activist Thich Nhat Hanh.

Training for Change
Website: www.trainingforchange.org
Email: info@trainingforchange.org
Address: PO Box 30914
Philadelphia, PA 19104
Phone: 267-289-2280

War Resisters' International
Website: http://wri-irg.org
Email: info@wri-irg.org
Address: 5 Caledonian Road, London, N1 9DX BRITAIN
Phone: +44-20-7278 4040
Fax: +44-20-7278 0444

Books, Articles, Films:

Why Civil Resistance Works, by Erica Chenoweth and Maria J. Stephan, available at Columbia University Press (See also: www.ericachenoweth.com)

The dilemma action: analysis of an activist technique, Majken Jul Sørensen and Brian Martin Published in *Peace & Change,* Volume 39, Number 1, January 2014, pp. 73-100

A Force More Powerful, documentary produced by Peter Ackerman and Jack Duvall, narrated by Ben Kingsley. www.aforcemorepowerful.org

A Force More Powerful, book by Peter Ackerman and Jack Duvall, available at www.palgrave.com/page/detail/a-force-more-powerful-peter-ackerman

The Handbook for Nonviolent Campaigns, War Resisters' International, available at www.wri-irg.org

Connect with Rivera Sun:

Rivera Sun
Website: www.riverasun.com
Email: rivera@riverasun.com
Facebook: Rivera Sun
Twitter: @RiveraSunAuthor

Appendix D: Table for Identifying Potential Constructive Programs

Fill in the chart with yes or no answers. You may wish to add notes below with further details. If all your answers to the questions are "yes" for a particular basic need, you may have a potential constructive program on your hands. Write "yes" in the last column. If your answers were predominately "no", then it is possible that this basic need is not a good candidate for a constructive program. If your answers were mixed, simply write "maybe" in the last column.

Questions:

- Is this basic need being fulfilled in our community or movement? Or is it lacking?
- Could fulfilling the need strengthen our movement?
- Does our community or movement depend on the opposition to fulfill this need? Would satisfying the need lessen our dependency on the opposition?
- Would fulfilling the need weaken our opposition?
- Does fulfilling the need directly resolve the issue or confront the current system that causes the issue?
- Can everyone participate?
- Is this basic need a good candidate for crafting a constructive program around?

Basic Need	Lacking in community?	Strengthens movement?	Lessens dependency?	Weakens opposition?	Confronts issue or system?	Can everyone participate?	Potential constructive program?
Food							
Shelter							
Clothing							
Water							
Money							
Energy							
Communication							
Information							
Education							
Entertainment							
Other							

Examples:

Example 1: Salt Satyagraha Constructive Program in India 1930
Issue: Indian Independence and Ending British Rule

Basic Need	Lacking in community?	Strengthens movement?	Lessens dependency?	Weakens opposition?	Confronts issue or system?	Can everyone participate?	Potential constructive program?
Salt	Yes (1)	Yes. (2)	Yes.	Yes. (3)	Yes. (4)	Yes.	Yes

(1) It is lacking in the communities because of British Salt Laws.
(2) It strengthens the Independence movement by increasing the Indian people's self-reliance and self-rule.
(3) Undermines British authority and control. Also, economically impacts their profits from salt.
(4) Effectively removes British power by mass noncooperation and civil disobedience of their laws.

Example 2: Local Solar Grids – people installing community-wide grids because the coal-based public utility refuses to change.

Basic Need	Lacking in community?	Strengthens movement?	Lessens dependency?	Weakens opposition?	Confronts issue or system?	Can everyone participate?	Potential constructive program?
Energy (Solar)	Yes. (1)	Maybe. (2)	Yes.	Yes.	Yes.	Yes. (Sort of) (3)	Maybe.

(1) Energy is not lacking in our community, but it is being provided in an unacceptable way (through coal).

(2) Installing our own local solar grids requires civil disobedience to the unjust laws that grant electrical utilities monopolies. This program would strengthen our movement by giving us energy self-reliance, but it might potentially weaken the movement if we do not plan to confront the legal challenges that will definitely ensue.

(3) Everyone can participate, although there is a technical aspect that requires assistance from solar engineers. Everyone can help with the manual labor of installing and maintaining the system, fundraising for the panels, and encouraging the community to participate.

Acknowledgements

My deepest gratitude goes out to the following people who lent me their insights, wisdom, statistics, charts, tables, graphics, quotes, research, photos, humor, and patience:

Dariel Garner, Tom Hastings, Les Reasonover; Jamila Raqib, Gene Sharp, and the Albert Einstein Institution; Michael Nagler, Stephanie Van Hook, and the Metta Center for Nonviolence; Philippe Duhamel, Erica Chenoweth, Mary Elizabeth King, Ivan Marovic, Rev. James Lawson, and the James Lawson Institute; Jack Duvall, Hardy Merriman, and the International Center on Nonviolent Conflict; George Lakey; Ken Butigan, John Dear, Veronica Pelicaric, and Pace e Bene's Campaign Nonviolence; and many others.

For photos and images, special thank you to: Grace Silvermoon, Shelly Johnson, Leah Cook, Velcrow Ripper, Dariel Garner, Nickie Sekera, Josie Lenwell, Wikimedia Commons, Rich Hillwig, David Geitgey Sierralupe, David Soumis, Martine Zee, Margaret Flowers and Kevin Zeese, Marirose Nightsong, Mona Caron, Philippe Duhamel, Erica Chenoweth, David Gibson, Bill Moeller, Ethan Au Green, Anita Stewart, Jerry Monroe Maynard, LJ Prip, Chas Schaeffer, Carol Brown, Brian Heater, Bill Moyer and Backbone Campaign, Jay Moore.

And, of course, a few giants whose shoulders we all stand on: Mohandas K. Gandhi, Dr. Martin Luther King, Jr., Dolores Huerta, Cesar Chavez, Dorothy Day, Alice Paul, Leo Tolstoy, Jesus, Siddhartha Buddha, and the most important "giant" of all: the millions of ordinary, extraordinary people who have brought us to today.

About Rivera Sun Novels, Workshops & Readings

Rivera Sun regularly teaches workshops on strategic nonviolent action. To connect with Rivera about a workshop, reading, or speaking event, please visit www.riverasun.com or email her at rivera@riverasun.com.

Billionaire Buddha

-the journey from fabulous wealth to unlimited blessings-
A powerful new novel from Rivera Sun, based on a true story! The price of enlightenment may bankrupt billionaire Dave Grant. Emotionally destitute in the prime of his career, he searches for love and collides with Joan Hathaway. The encounter rattles his soul and unravels his world. Capitalism, property, wealth, mansions: his notions of success crumble into dust. From toasting champagne on top of the world to swigging whiskey with bums in the gutter, Dave Grant's journey is an unforgettable ride that turns everyone's world upside down!

The Dandelion Insurrection

"When fear is used to control us, love is how we rebel!" Under a gathering storm of tyranny, Zadie Byrd Gray whirls into the life of Charlie Rider and asks him to become the voice of the Dandelion Insurrection. With the rallying cry of life, liberty, and love, Zadie and Charlie fly across America leaving a wake of revolution in their path. Passion erupts. Danger abounds. The lives of millions hang by a thin thread of courage, but in the midst of the madness, the golden soul of humanity blossoms . . . and miracles start to unfold!

Steam Drills, Treadmills, and Shooting Stars

A soaring tribute to the beauty of the human spirit! The ghost of John Henry haunts Jack Dalton, a coal company lawyer, and challenges him to stand up to the steam drills of contemporary America. Meanwhile, young Henrietta Owens, activist and mother, captivates the nation with some tough-loving truth about the environment, the economy, justice and hope.

Order novels through any major online bookstore or from Rivera Sun at www.riverasun.com

Author/Actress Rivera Sun sings the anthem of our times and rallies us to meet adversity with gusto. She is the author of three social protest novels, *The Dandelion Insurrection, Billionaire Buddha,* and *Steam Drills, Treadmills, and Shooting Stars*, as well as nine theatrical plays, a book of poetry, and this study guide. Rivera cohosts Occupy Radio, and cofounded the nationwide nonviolent study and action group network, the Love-in-Action Network. She is the social media director for Pace e Bene/ Campaign Nonviolence, and her essays on social justice have appeared in Truthout.org, and Popular Resistance.org, among other publications. She attended the James Lawson Institute on Strategic Nonviolent Conflict in 2014. She went to Bennington College to study writing as a Harcourt Scholar and graduated with a degree in dance. After six years working as a professional playwright, choreographer, and director in the San Francisco Bay Area, she founded the nationally touring Rising Sun Dance & Theater company. In 2010, Rivera Sun wrote and performed a trilogy of solo theater shows entitled *The Freedom Stories of Lala* that received coast-to-coast standing ovations. Rivera lives in an earthship house in Taos, New Mexico, where she grows tomatoes and bakes sourdough bread in an adobe oven. She has red hair, a twin sister, and a fondness for esoteric mystics. Everything else about her – except her writing – is perfectly ordinary.

Connect with Rivera Sun:
Website: www.riverasun.com
Email: rivera@riverasun.com
Facebook: Rivera Sun
Twitter: @RiveraSunAuthor

Made in the USA
San Bernardino, CA
13 December 2019

61425332R00071